D1532214

# The Infused Palate

## *Cooking with Extra Virgin Olive Oils and Balsamic Vinegars*

Eileen Sanger Profit

Printed by Printing Plus Graphic Design Inc.
Text copyright 2012
For information please contact sangerartist@optonline.net
ISBN # 978-0-692-01897-2

#  Contents

#  *Acknowledgments*

*I would like to thank my loving husband Freddy and my beautiful, loving daughter Kristen for putting up with my many successes and failures.  Love you both!*

*A special thanks to Mona, Bob and Dana for helping me to discover their amazing Extra Virgin Olive Oils and Balsamic Vinegars and allowing me to work for them.  It's been a joy!*

*To my friends and family who give me constant support.  I feel blessed.*

*And finally to my mother, although you are not here on earth, I feel you always. Rest in Peace!*

1

# Introduction

"Something smells good. What are you cooking?" are some of the comments from my guests as they enter my home. Let's be honest. Most of us would like to create a meal that would not only look and taste great but also wow our guests.

Just a little background, I am not a chef, I did not go to culinary school and I did not work for a restaurant. I am an artist and a passionate cook. I was an avid viewer of the French Chef cooking series on public television many years ago. I love reading cookbooks, shopping for meals. and eating the final results. I enjoy putting flavors together and planning a menu where each course enhances the next. I love to set a beautiful table and plate artistically. I love to entertain friends and family and I love the stimulating conversations that happen because of wonderful food and good wine.

A year ago I began working in a tasting and retail shop that features fine flavored extra virgin olive oils and balsamic vinegars. Once rare, these specialty shops are becoming more and more common. In these shops the consumer gets to taste the products before they buy. The products will vary in each store, but the oils and vinegars are award winning products sourced from around the world. The quality and variety available are amazing and this exposure has been a revelation for my own cooking.

I began incorporating these products in my own kitchen and loved the new tastes. I began bringing samples of dishes I was making to the shop for customers to taste. I would share the recipe along with the samples. The customers were also excited about how the addition of these flavored oils and vinegars made food better and loved having recipes. The success of my samples led to this book.

This book is a collection of many recipes I developed to incorporate these incredible tastes in your meals. Most of the recipes in this book are easily prepared and can be made in under an hour. The more complicated recipes that take some time, I think are worth the effort and can be done for special occasions or on a day when you have time to cook. I have broken the cookbook down into chapters with some cook's notes to help with your meal planning and to offer some alternatives in case your family and friends have particular tastes.

In addition to the recipes, I have included health information about the oils and vinegars, storage information, and buying tips. There are ideas for glazes etc. in the back of the book along with a suggested menu planner. At the end of the book you will find blank pages so you can add your own notes. Change or add to the recipes as you go along. It's always fun to look back and see when you first cooked a recipe and how you personalized it.

I hope this book will help you cook with olive oils and balsamic vinegars and make the experience of cooking fun. Why shouldn't cooking be pleasurable? Isn't it a sensual experience? It reaches your sense of smell, taste, touch and sight. I enjoy the whole experience of cooking and I hope you do as well.
Thomas Keller, master chef and restaurateur, once wrote, ".... to make people happy, that is what cooking is about."

Comparing Recipes with My Friend Colleen

# *Health Benefits of Extra Virgin Olive Oil*

**Extra Virgin Olive Oil** is a super food. It is obtained from the fruit of olive trees. The term extra virgin means the oil has been obtained from the original fruit and has not been synthetically treated. Immediately after harvest these olives are pressed, washed, and centrifuged to extract the oil. The oil is then decanted and filtered. This is the finest quality of olive oil and has powerful effects on your health. The Mediterranean diet is the healthiest diet in the world, something the Greeks and Italians have known for centuries, and always includes an ample amount of olive oil, the main source of fat, for health reasons and taste. Just about every recipe in this cookbook has extra virgin olive oil as an ingredient. The flavored oils are so tasty and add so much to the food that you forget how incredibly healthy it is for you. Here are a few facts about extra virgin olive oil:

**Rich in Vitamins A, B-1, B-2, C, D, E, K and iron**

**Lowers harmful LDL cholesterol**

**Decreases risk of Cardiovascular Disease**

**Reduces high blood pressure**

**Lowers triglyceride levels**

**Dissolves clots in capillaries**

**Lessons the severity of asthma and arthritis**

**Is a natural anti-inflammatory (same ingredient as found in ibuprofen)**

**Reduces risk of Alzheimer's disease**

**Inhibits the growth of some cancers**

Aids in digestion and controls blood sugar levels

Helps to maintain a lower body weight

Treats urinary and bladder infections

Fights against acne, psoriasis, and eczema

# *Cooking and Baking with Extra Virgin Olive Oil*

Extra virgin olive oils should be used for finishing, cooking and baking. The healthy fats in olive oil make it the better choice and are becoming a staple in many kitchens. Many chefs and cooks around the country use extra virgin olive oils in their recipes. You can cook and should cook anything with extra virgin olive oil. You can use it for dipping, sautéing and light frying or you can pour it over rice, vegetables, meats and potatoes as a finish or use it in soups, pastas, stews, or anything you prepare. Olive oil is a great choice and adds aroma and depth to all food. The most important thing is to find an olive oil that tastes great to you. The flavor will shine through.

There has been much discussion about the use of extra virgin olive oil for frying. Olive oil has a high smoke point, which means the temperature at which the oil begins to break down and smoke. Extra virgin olive oil can actually be used for frying because the smoke point is generally between 375 and 410 degrees Fahrenheit which cover many forms of cooking. Remember to bring the olive oil up to heat gradually. This will prevent burning and will keep the oil at optimum heat without a reaction.

Baking with olive oil can replace melted butter, vegetable oil, canola oil or many other oils in recipes. The addition of extra virgin olive oil in baking reduces the cholesterol and saturated fat count. It adds more flavors and makes baked goods moist and lighter tasting. There is a conversion chart for butter to olive oil in the back of the book. Use this guide to replace melted butter in recipes.

Using a high quality fresh extra virgin olive oil in cooking and baking is the best way to enhance your heath and create delicious meals.

There was a wonderful article in one of the papers, and I can't remember who wrote it but the content was intriguing. The editor stated that on one of the food blogs he visited someone wrote in that olive oil is dangerous when it is heated and that it somehow turns into a harmful trans fat.
The replied comment by the editor was," you could no more produce a trans fat in your home kitchen than you could refine crude petroleum into gas for your car."

# *Storing Extra Virgin Olive Oil*

Freshness is the key to great olive oil.  The extra virgin olive oils suggested in these recipes are of the highest quality. Our distributor imports over a million gallons of premium extra virgin olive oil every year.  To maintain freshness he imports many varieties of olive oils from small producing estates from all over the world. These change according to the time of harvest from the Northern and Southern hemispheres.  Our distributor is fussy about the way he handles these oils. He assures the products health benefits by abiding by his strict rule of freshness first. This insures the consumer is purchasing the finest oil money can buy.

Unlike wine, olive oil does not improve with age.  It is a natural fruit and must be handled with care.  The enemy of olive oil is light, air and age.  Good quality olive oil is protected from light by placing it in dark bottles.  Once bottled these oils should be used within a year. Store your extra virgin olive oil in a pantry or cabinet away from heat and light to maintain its freshness.   Every month the olive oil is stored the acidity levels increase as a result of oxidation.  Extra virgin olive oil has a longer shelf life because they start out with a lower acidity level. Make sure the tops fit tightly to insure freshness.  Do not store olive oil in plastic containers. The oil will be compromised from the harmful substances in plastic.

Olive oil should not be refrigerated.  Its optimum flavor is realized when it is at room temperature.  Cold temperatures could create condensation in the oil and could spoil the oil's flavor or cause rancidity.  It will also make the oil cloudy which will clear up again at room temperature.

Personal taste, the oils freshness and the way the store treats their oils is the best way for you as the consumer to purchase extra virgin olive oils.  After all, it's your hard earned money!

# *Health Benefits of Balsamic Vinegars*

**Balsamic Vinegars** are made from the pressing of grapes. They are placed into wooden kegs and go through a natural aging process which can take many years. These balsamics from Modena are the most sought after balsamics. The natural fermentation produces a thick substance with many health benefits. The same substance, polyphenols, which is found in extra virgin olive oils is also found in balsamic vinegars. This antioxidant is powerful. Here are a few facts about balsamic vinegar:

**Protects the heart from heart disease and cancer**

**Improves immune system**

**Guards against harmful radicals**

**Suppresses the body's appetite**

**Rich in potassium, manganese, calcium and iron**

**Regulates blood sugar**

**Helps to strengthen bones**

**Anti-viral and anti bacterial qualities**

**Reduces high blood pressure**

**Reduces acne**

**Prevents anemia**

**Reduces inception of headaches**

#  *Cooking and Baking with Balsamic Vinegars*

Good quality aged **Balsamic Vinegars** and Infused balsamics, made in Modena, are the most sought after vinegars. Balsamic vinegars are made from a reduction of grapes and the juice is natural and unfermented. Reputable tasting rooms treat their balsamics with care by storing them in stainless steel containers called fusti's and pouring your selection into dark bottles.   Unlike extra virgin olive oils, oxygen is not a problem for balsamic. There is no need to refrigerate and once the bottle is opened it can be stored indefinitely in a cool, dark place, away from heat and light.

Balsamics add flavor and depth to many dishes. It's not just for salads, although the flavored balsamics make incredibly tasty vinaigrettes.  There are many recipes in this book that incorporate the use of these vinegars. Below are a few more suggestions on how to use your aged and infused balsamics.

Try different flavors over Parmigianino Reggiano cheese

Finishing sauce for fish, grilled vegetables, fried calamari, risottos, and pastas

Add to omelets, casseroles, sauces, soups and stews

On ice cream and fruits

Use in marinades for fish, meats, poultry and vegetables

Substitute half of the vinegar in a recipe with balsamic vinegar

Substitute ¼ of the lemon juice or lime in a recipe with a citrus balsamic

Try balsamics in salads without oil

There are many more ways to use your creativity.  Pair your balsamics with different extra virgin olive oils to enhance your favorite dishes.  Use the pairing chart in the back of the book for more ideas.

Olives, Olives, and More Olives

#  *Appetizers/Starters*

| | |
|---|---|
| 17 | Marinated Olives |
| 18 | Melon with Prosciutto |
| 19 | Tomato Bruschetta with Gorgonzola |
| 20 | Fig Tapenade and Mascarpone Cheese |
| 21 | Goat Cheese Apple Puffs |
| 22 | Pumpkin Butter and Goat Cheese Crostini |
| 23 | Balsamic Onion Baked Brie |
| 24 | Sausage and Leek Tart |
| 25 | Deviled Eggs with Truffle Oil |
| 27 | Crab Cakes with Aioli |
| 29 | Caprese Salad Appetizer |
| 30 | Oven Toasted Tomatoes, Pesto and Goat Cheese Torta |

#  *Marinated Olives*

*I love olives.  To me they are a snack.  I enjoy them alone, with Italian antipasti, in salads and also in pasta.  They are especially good when they are marinated in herbs.*

**Makes about 1 1/2 cups**

4 oz. green olives
8 oz. Kalamata olives
1 Tbs. lemon zest
1 Tbs. orange zest
1 tsp. dried thyme or 1 Tbs. fresh minced thyme
1 clove garlic minced
1 Tbs. minced fresh rosemary
1/8  tsp. Red pepper flakes.
2 -3 Tbs. **Nocellara del Belice, Arbosana, Sicilian Blend, Manzanillo, or Picholine Extra Virgin Oil**

Combine all ingredients in a bowl.  Keep refrigerated for at least a day before serving.  You can put olives in an airtight jar in refrigerator.   Always let olives come to room temperature before serving.

# *Melon with Prosciutto*

*This is a refreshing and flavorful appetizer. It's light enough to serve before any dinner or lunch menu. Use a ripe cantaloupe.*

½ ripe cantaloupe, peeled, seeds removed
2 oz. prosciutto, sliced
4 fresh figs, quartered
Few sprigs of mint
3 Tbs. **Fig Balsamic Vinegar**

Cut cantaloupe into ¼" wedges. Slice prosciutto into long thin slices and wrap around center of melon wedges. Place on platter. Scatter fig pieces and drizzle entire plate with the balsamic. Place mint sprigs to decorate.

**Cook's Note**
If you can't find fresh figs you can omit them. If you prefer to reduce the balsamic to a glaze the directions are in back of book. You have the option of using it straight from the bottle.

# *Tomato Bruschetta with Gorgonzola*

*All I can say about this recipe is wow! The flavors are incredible. Makes a great appetizer when sliced into smaller portions or have it in a larger portion as a light dinner with a glass of wine.*

**Serves 6-8**

1 loaf Italian bread
¼ cup **Garlic Extra Virgin Olive Oil**
5 vine ripe red tomatoes
2 vine ripe yellow tomatoes
½ teaspoon salt
¼ teaspoon pepper
¼ cup chopped fresh basil leaves
¼ cup **18 Year Aged Balsamic Vinegar**
½ cup **Nocellara Extra Virgin Olive Oil**
¼ cup finely sliced red onion
6 oz. crumbled gorgonzola cheese

Cut bread in half lengthwise. Brush both pieces with olive oil and cut each half into 4 equal pieces. Place bread in hot skillet, brushed side down to toast until slightly browned. Cut tomatoes in half then into 6 wedges each half. Place in large bowl. Add basil leaves and stir gently. Add salt and pepper. Add balsamic vinegar and ¼ cup of Nocellara olive oil. Mix gently. To serve, put slice of toasted bread on platter. Top with a few sliced onions, then tomato mixture followed by a generous sprinkling of gorgonzola. (If you like the cheese slightly melted, you can place under a broiler for about 1 minute.)

**Cook's Note**
I like my bread a little soggy so I add a little liquid from the tomato mixture onto the bread. It also makes it easier to cut with a knife when eating. If you can't find yellow tomatoes, all red would be fine. Any good Sicilian Extra Virgin Olive Oil can replace Nocellara.

# Fig Tapenade and Mascarpone Crostini

*If you enjoy the flavor of figs you will enjoy this tapenade. There are many ingredients in this recipe but it is quite simple to make and worth the effort.*

1 cup mission figs (stems removed)
1/3 cup water
1/3 cup chopped Kalamata olives
2 Tbs. **Eureka Lemon Extra Virgin Olive Oil**
2 Tbs. **Fig Balsamic Vinegar**
½ tsp. lemon juice
1 Tbs. drained capers
1 ½ tsp. chopped fresh thyme leaves
½ tsp. garlic powder
½ tsp. salt
1 loaf French Baguette cut into ¼" slices
**Garlic Extra Virgin Olive Oil** for brushing
8 oz. container Mascarpone, room temperature
Prosciutto slices (optional)

In a heavy saucepan combine figs with water. Cook over medium heat for about 5 minutes until water has evaporated. Transfer to food processor. Add the next 7 ingredients and pulse until chopped but not pureed. Remove to a bowl and season with salt. Cover and let sit overnight in refrigerator. Preheat oven to 375 degrees. Arrange bread slices on baking sheet and brush lightly with the garlic olive oil. Place in oven on center rack and bake about 8 – 10 minutes until edges are golden. Let cool. Spread slices with mascarpone and top with tapenade mixture. Add a small slice of prosciutto if desired.

**Cook's Note**
You may substitute Mascarpone with Cream Cheese, or Ricotta Cheese. For extra sweetness, drizzle tops of crostini with more of the Fig Balsamic.

# Goat Cheese Apple Puffs

*These are easily prepared cocktail party hors d'oeuvres. If you don't have a biscuit cutter you can cut dough into 1- 1 ½"squares.*

**Serves 8**

2 sheets frozen puff pastry sheets (thawed in refrigerator)
3 ounces softened goat cheese
3 Tbs. heavy cream
¼ cup Apple Butter
1 Tbs. **Red Apple Balsamic Vinegar**
1 tsp. dried rosemary
Salt and pepper
1 egg beaten

Preheat oven to 400 degrees. Remove pastry from refrigerator and working with one sheet at a time, roll out to about 15" x 15" on a floured board. In a bowl mix softened goat cheese with cream until smooth. Spread goat cheese over pastry. In a small bowl mix apple butter with balsamic until incorporated. Spread on top of goat cheese layer. Sprinkle with rosemary. Sprinkle lightly with salt and pepper. Put aside. Roll out second sheet of pastry dough to the same size as the first sheet and gently place over top of prepared sheet. Use fingers or rolling pin to pat down layer, making sure it is sealed well. Use a 1-1 ½ " round cookie cutter or biscuit cutter to cut out shapes. Place on baking sheet lined with parchment paper. Brush tops with egg and bake in oven for 10-15 minutes until puffed and lightly browned. Remove from oven and cool to room temperature. Puffs can be reheated in oven at 350 degrees for 5 minutes.

# *Pumpkin Butter and Goat Cheese Crostini*

*This is a great appetizer. It is easy to make and the flavors together are delicious. It is also great on a buffet table.*

1 loaf French baguette, cut into ¼" thick slices
¼ cup **Tuscan Herb Extra Virgin Olive Oil**
5.5 oz. log goat cheese softened to room temperature
½ - ¾ cup **Braswell's Pumpkin Butter**
¼ cup chopped pecans, lightly toasted
3 scallions, finely chopped
3 Tbs. cooked, drained, chopped bacon (optional)

Preheat oven to 400 degrees. Place slices of baguette on baking sheet in single layer. Brush one side of bread with the olive oil and toast in the oven for 10 minutes, until golden on edges. Let cool completely. When ready to serve spread goat cheese on each slice and top with layer of spread pumpkin butter. Sprinkle each with chopped pecans and scallions. If you do not use the bacon then lightly salt each one.

**Cook's Note**
If you can't find pumpkin butter, sweet potato or apple butter will do. Prosciutto can be substituted for the bacon.

# *Balsamic Onion Baked Brie*

*One of my most enjoyable foods is brie.  I love the creaminess and the taste.  This appetizer is definitely for brie lovers.  It is an incredible tasting appetizer and has a wonderful presentation.*

Serves 6

½ cup **Braswells Balsamic Sweet Onion Jam**
2 Tbs. **Wild Mushroom and Sage Extra Virgin Olive Oil**
1 tsp. minced fresh rosemary
1 (15oz.) wheel Brie cheese
1 French baguette cut into ¼ "sliced and toasted

In a bowl combine jam, olive oil and rosemary.  Mix well to incorporate.  Cut a thin slice off top of brie and sides to remove the rind and expose the cheese.  Place cheese on a deep plate and spread the jam mixture evenly over the top of cheese.  Cook in microwave for 1 minute or until cheese melts slightly.  Serve immediately with the baquette toasts or melba crackers.

**Cook's Note**
You may substitute with Porcini Extra Virgin Olive Oil, Eureka Lemon Extra Virgin Olive Oil, or Basil Extra Virgin Olive Oil.  If you can't find Braswell's Onion Jam you will find the recipe the recipe for Balsamic Onion Marmalade on page 131.

# *Sausage and Leek Tart*

*This is a delicious tart which can be made with a prepared frozen pie shell. It can be served at breakfast, as a nice component for a buffet, or as an appetizer before a meal.*

1 frozen prepared 9" pie shell, defrosted
3 medium leeks, washed thoroughly
1 Tbs. **Herbs de Provence Extra Virgin Olive Oil**
5 breakfast link sausages
½ cup grated Fontina cheese
½ cup grated Gruyere cheese
4 large eggs
2/3 cup heavy cream
¼ tsp. salt
Dash of nutmeg
1 Tbs. butter

Preheat oven to 375 degrees. Place pie weights in prepared pie shell and bake for 5 minutes. Remove from oven and take out weights. Slice leeks into ¼" rounds using white part only. Place olive oil in pan and cook leeks for 8-10 minutes until soft. Remove to a bowl. Using same pan, add sausages and brown until done. Add a little more olive oil if needed. Remove and let cool slightly. Cut sausages lengthwise to create 10 halves and set aside. In another bowl whisk together, eggs, cream, salt and nutmeg. Stir in leeks and cheeses. Pour into prepared pie shell and place sausages on top. Bake 30-40 minutes until golden brown and cake tester comes out clean when inserted into center. Serve warm

# Deviled Eggs with Truffle Oil

*These are great appetizers for a buffet table. The trick in this dish is to cook the eggs properly. If you love the combination of truffle oil and eggs, then you'll love this dish.*

**Makes 24**

12 large eggs, room temperature
5 Tbs. good quality mayonnaise
2 tsp. **Sicilian Lemon Balsamic Vinegar**
1 Tbs. Dijon mustard
1 Tbs. **White Truffle Oil**
1 Tbs. finely chopped chives plus more for decoration
Pinch of salt pinch of cayenne pepper

Put eggs in a large pot and fill with cold water about 1" above eggs. Bring eggs to a boil over high heat. Cover the pot and turn off heat. Let eggs sit in pot for 10 minutes. Carefully remove eggs and immediately place in a large bowl with ice water. Let eggs sit in water for 5 minutes until cooled. Remove eggs and peel them under cool running tap water. (This makes it easier to remove the shell). Slice the peeled eggs in half and remove egg yolks. Place egg white halves on a flat dish and place egg yolks in a bowl. Mash eggs yolks with a fork and add the mayonnaise, vinegar, mustard, truffle oil, chives, salt and cayenne pepper. Taste and add more truffle oil and salt if needed. Put the egg mixture into a piping bag. Pipe the mixture into the egg white halves and garnish with some chopped chives.

**Cook's Note**
If you don't have a piping bag you can use a zip lock bag. Fill the bag with the egg mixture and snip a small hole in the bottom corner of the bag. Pipe the mixture into the egg whites.

# *Crab Cakes with Aioli*

*Crab cakes are always a great appetizer for a buffet, luncheon or sit down meal. These are nice and moist. Choose your favorite aioli.*

Serves 4 to 6

1 lb. crabmeat, picked over
½ cup finely chopped celery
¼ cup finely chopped green onions
1 cup fine bread crumbs
1 large egg beaten
¼ cup good quality mayonnaise
1 Tbs. **Sicilian Lemon Balsamic Vinegar**
1 Tbs. Dijon mustard
1 Tbs. finely chopped parsley
2 tsp. fine chopped cilantro (optional)
Dash cayenne pepper
½ tsp. salt
¾ cup panko breadcrumbs
3 Tblsp. **Milanese Gremolata Extra Virgin Olive Oil**

## Chipotle Aioli
½ cup good quality mayonnaise
2 Tbs. **Chipotle Extra Virgin Olive Oil**
1 Tbs. fresh lime juice
1 small garlic clove, minced
Salt if needed

## Lemon Aioli
½ cup good quality mayonnaise
1 Tbs. minced green onions
½ tsp. lemon zest
2 Tbs. **Eureka Lemon Extra Virgin Olive Oil**
Salt if needed

Combine crabmeat, celery, green onions, bread crumbs, beaten egg, mayonnaise, balsamic vinegar, Dijon mustard, parsley, cilantro and cayenne pepper. Mix gently. Add salt if needed. Shape into 8 to 12 cakes. Place panko breadcrumbs on a flat dish and coat crab cakes evenly. Heat olive oil in a non stick skillet over medium high heat. Add crab cakes. Do not over crowd. (You might have to cook them in 2 batches). Cook for about 4 minutes on one side and carefully turn crab cakes and cook another 4 minutes. Serve with your choice of aioli.
To make aioli, put all ingredients in a bowl and mix well.

**Footnote**
You can use egg substitute in place of the egg.

# *Caprese Salad Appetizer*

*This shouts summer with fresh ripe tomatoes, fresh basil and homemade mozzarella with a drizzle of the best extra virgin olive oil and balsamic glaze. What could be better?*

Serves 4-6

2 lbs. vine ripe tomatoes, sliced ¼" thick
1 lb. fresh mozzarella, sliced ¼" thick
¼ to ½ cup packed fresh basil leaves
3 to 4 Tbs. **Nocellara del Belice Extra Virgin Olive Oil**
salt if needed
**18 Year Aged Balsamic Vinegar** glaze for drizzling

Place a tomato slice, a basil leaf, and a slice of mozzarella, on a platter or an individual plate, alternating ingredients in that matter in a circular pattern until platter is full. Sprinkle with lightly with salt. Drizzle with olive oil. Drizzle balsamic glaze over top, dot around plate, or make crisscross patterns over top of salad. You can also choose to stack the ingredients which make a nice individual presentation.

**Cook's Note**
The authentic Italian version does not include balsamic glaze. But honestly, who can refuse!
This glaze can be kept in a container or in an airtight bottle on the counter. The recipe is on page 132.

29

# *Oven Roasted Tomatoes, Pesto and Goat Cheese Torta*

*I dare you to stop eating these after your first bite. The true Italian flavors just send your taste buds into ecstasy. This is a fabulous buffet appetizer and great for parties.*

**Serves 6-8**

2 tsp. **Tuscan Herb Extra Virgin Olive Oil**
10 – 12 Slow Roasted Tomato halves (recipe page 129)
¼ cup basil oil pesto (recipe page 125)
4 oz. cream cheese or mascarpone cheese, softened
4 oz. goat cheese softened
8-10 fresh basil leaves
French baguette
2-3 Tbs. **Garlic Extra Virgin Olive Oil**

Place a large piece of plastic wrap to fit inside a 2 cup bowl. Leave enough wrap on sides to cover top later. Brush the olive oil over inside of plastic. Mix cream cheese and goat cheese in a small bowl. Place 4 or 5 basil leaves into bottom of bowl lined with plastic wrap. Spread ½ of the goat cheese mixture on top. Place 5 to 6 roasted tomatoes on top making sure goat cheese is covered well. Spread ½ of pesto on top. Repeat order using rest of goat cheese tomato and pesto. Finish by topping it with 4 or 5 basil leaves. Fold excess plastic wrap over top, covering well. Lightly press down. Place in refrigerator for 2 hours. Meanwhile preheat oven to 400 degrees. Cut baguette into ¼" slices and place on baking sheet. Brush with garlic oil and place in oven for about 8 minutes or until edges are barely light brown. Remove and let cool. Remove torta from refrigerator and undo plastic wrap on top. Invert onto a platter and remove plastic wrap. Serve with baguette slices.

#  Soups

# *Cream of Wild Mushroom Soup*

*This is a velvety mushroom soup. It is a great winter comfort food. You may use vegetable broth in place of the meat broths, keeping this soup vegetarian.*

**Serves 6**

½ oz. dried porcini mushrooms
6 oz. Shitake mushrooms
1 lb. Portobello mushrooms
3 Tbs. unsalted butter
3 Tbs. **Porcini Extra Virgin Olive Oil**
1 cup finely chopped shallots
2 garlic cloves, finely chopped
2 tsp. chopped fresh thyme leaves
1 tsp. chopped fresh rosemary
1 tsp. chopped fresh sage
¼ cup chopped parsley
2 Tbs. dry sherry
2 Tbs. all purpose flour
2 (14.5 oz) cans low salt chicken broth
1 (14.5 oz) can low salt beef broth
1 Tbs. **18 Year Aged Balsamic Vinegar**
½ cup heavy cream
Salt and pepper
**Eureka Lemon Extra Virgin Olive Oil**

**Cook's Note**
Replace the heavy cream with half and half to save calories. You can use Mushroom Sage Extra Virgin Olive Oil in place of the Porcini Olive Oil.

Boil ½ cup water in a small saucepan. Add dried porcini mushrooms, stir and remove from heat. Let rest in saucepan for 15 minutes. Meanwhile, clean Shitake and Portobello mushrooms and cut into 1/8 to ¼" slices and set aside. Put butter and oil in a pot over medium heat. Add shallots and sauté for 3 minutes. Add garlic and continue to sauté for 1 minute more. Add sliced mushrooms and herbs and sauté until softened and slightly browned, about 8 minutes. (Do not burn). Add sherry, stirring until liquid is almost evaporated. Add flour and stir to incorporate for about 2 minutes. Stir in broth and balsamic vinegar. Strain porcini mushrooms over a bowl, reserving liquid. Chop porcini mushrooms and add to soup along with its broth. Bring to a boil, then reduce and simmer the soup uncovered for about 30 minutes. Remove from heat. Ladle soup into a food processor and pulse in batches until soup is finely pureed. Add soup back into pot and cook over medium low heat, while stirring in heavy cream. Combine well until heated through. Add salt and pepper to taste. Serve in bowls and decorate with parsley leaves and a drizzle of the lemon olive oil.

# Carrot Tarragon Soup

*This is a lovely soup for any time of year which can be served hot or cold. For a vegetarian version use the vegetable broth in place of chicken broth.*

*Serves 6*

2 lbs. carrots, peeled and chopped
1 large onion chopped
3 cloves garlic, minced
3 Tbs. **Tarragon Extra Virgin Olive Oil**
5 cups low salt chicken broth or vegetable broth
1 tsp. freshly grated ginger
½ cup fresh orange juice
1 heaping Tbs. fresh tarragon, finely chopped
1 tsp. cumin
Salt and pepper to taste
½ cup sour cream, room temperature
2 Tbs. chopped chives

In a large pot add olive oil, carrots, onion and garlic. Cover and cook on medium heat until onions are translucent and carrots are slightly tender, about 10 minutes, stirring occasionally. Add broth and bring to a boil. Reduce heat and add ginger and orange juice and stir until incorporated. Cover and continue cooking on low-medium heat for another 15-20 minutes or until carrots are completely tender. Let cool slightly and pour into a food processor or blender and blend until mixture is smooth. Transfer to a clean pot and add tarragon and cumin. Cover and cook over low heat or until heated through. Taste and add salt and pepper as needed. To serve, divide into soup bowls, add a teaspoon or two of sour cream swirled on surface of soup. Top with chopped chives.

# *Onion Soup with Pastry Crust*

*This is a twist on French onion soup. The combination of the onions, pastry and cheese make this soup the perfect comfort food.*

2 Tbs. unsalted butter
2 Tbs. **Herbs de Provence Extra Virgin Olive Oil**
3 large Vidalia onions, thinly sliced
1 Tbs. all purpose flour
4 cups beef stock or low sodium beef broth
1 cup water
1 bay leaf
2 tsp. dried thyme
1 Tbs. **18 Year Aged Balsamic Vinegar**
½ cup dry red wine
2 Tbs. cognac
Salt and pepper
Frozen puff pastry, at room temperature
1 ½ cup grated gruyere
½ cup grated Parmesan Cheese
1 egg, beaten slightly

Melt butter and olive oil in a large saucepan or sauté pan over medium heat. Add onions and cook uncovered, stirring, occasionally, until soft and golden brown, about 30-40 minutes. Add flour and stir for about 1 minute. Stir in stock, water, bay leaf, thyme, balsamic, wine, cognac, and simmer uncovered for about 30 minutes, stirring occasionally. Taste for salt and pepper. While soup is cooking prepare pastry. Preheat oven to 400 degrees. Place 1 pastry sheet on a lightly floured board and sprinkle with Parmesan cheese mixed with ½ cup of the grated Gruyere cheese. Place second pastry sheet on top and roll out to a 14" x 14" sheet. Cut out four 5" circles (Use a saucer plate as your template and cut around outside onto pastry). Divide soup into 4 ovenproof soup crocks. Sprinkle rest of cheese over the 4 soups. Cover with pastry lids and push down along edges to secure to the sides of the crocks. Brush with egg. Place crocks on a baking sheet and bake for about 15 minutes or until pastry is golden in color. Serve immediately.

# *Cauliflower and Leek Soup*

*This is a creamy soup and the addition of the scallops is an unexpected treat. This soup is elegant and perfect for a first course when entertaining.*

**Serves 6**

2 Tbs. **Garlic Extra Virgin Olive Oil**
1 medium onion, chopped
3 leeks, washed, sliced, white part only
1 large head cauliflower
4 cups low salt chicken stock or broth
½ cup heavy cream
6 large sea scallops
1 Tbs. butter
2 Tbs. **Eureka Lemon Extra Virgin Olive Oil**
Fresh chopped chives

Heat 1 Tbs. olive oil in a large pot over medium heat. Add onion and leeks and sauté about 5 minutes or until onions are soft. Season with salt and pepper. Chop cauliflower into bite size pieces and add to onions. Stir and immediately add broth and cream and bring to boil. Reduce heat to low, partially cover, and simmer until cauliflower is tender 20-25 minutes. Puree in food processor. Season with salt and pepper. Clean out pot and return puree to pot. Set aside. Heat butter and l Tbs. garlic olive oil in skillet. Dry scallops with paper towels and sprinkle with salt and pepper. Sear scallops in skillet until brown, about 1 ½ minutes each side. Remove and keep warm. Heat up soup. Ladle soup into individual bowls and place scallop in center of soup. Drizzle a little lemon oil around scallop on top of soup. Sprinkle soup with a small amount of chives.

**Cook's Note**
For an earthier taste, replace Lemon Extra Virgin Olive Oil with Truffle Oil.

# *Corn and Scallop Chowder*

*This soup is best when tomatoes are ripe and corn is fresh. It's a great summer soup. Serve this with a salad on the side and some crusty bread!*

**Serves 6**

4 oz. smoky bacon cut into 1" pieces
1 Tbs. **Basil Extra Virgin Olive Oil**
1 medium onion chopped
1 1b. sea scallops cut in 1" pieces
2 medium tomatoes, peeled, seeds removed and diced
1 cup half and half
1 cup heavy cream
6 whole ears of corn (kernels removed)
1 ( 8oz.) bottle clam juice
Pinch of red pepper flakes
2 drops tobasco
1 tsp. Worcestershire sauce
¼ tsp. liquid smoke (optional)
2 Tbs. butter
4 large leaves of basil, julienned
Salt and pepper to taste

Cook bacon in pot until soft and lightly brown. Remove with a slotted spoon and drain on paper towels. Set aside. Remove all but 1 teaspoon of bacon fat, add basil oil to pot and onions and sauté until translucent, about 5-8 minutes. Remove to a bowl. Add scallops and sauté over medium heat, about 2 minutes per side. Remove and set aside with onions and bacon. Pour half and half, heavy cream, tomatoes, corn and clam juice in pot. Simmer uncovered about 10 minutes. Be careful not to boil. Add the scallops, bacon and onion back into the pot and cook another 5-10 minutes. Just before serving, add the red pepper flakes, tobasco, liquid smoke, butter and basil. Stir, .taste and add salt and pepper if needed. Serve hot.

**Cook's Note**
You can replace the bacon with Chorizo sausage cut into ¼" slices. You may not need the red pepper flakes since the chorizo is hot and spicy.

# *Curried Tomato Soup with Croutons*

*Vegetarian comfort food. The warm creamy soup and the crunch of the croutons are very special. This soup can be served hot or cold so it makes it a great all around crowd pleaser.*

Serves 4-6

2 Tbs. Butter
**2 Tbs. Roasted Onion and Cilantro Extra Virgin Olive Oil**
1 large onion, chopped
4 garlic cloves, chopped
2 (28 oz.) can diced tomatoes with puree
or 4 ½ lbs. ripe tomatoes, peeled and diced
¼ cup tomato paste
3 cups vegetable stock
1 bay leaf
3 tsp. curry powder
1 tsp. coriander
1 tsp. cumin
1 tsp. salt
¼ cup chopped fresh cilantro
¾ cup half and half
Fresh pepper to taste

## Croutons
4 slices country style crusty bread
3 Tbs. **Roasted Onion and Cilantro Extra Virgin Olive Oil**
Salt and Pepper

Melt butter with oil in a large pot. Add onions and cook over medium heat until soft but not brown. Add garlic and cook for 2 minutes more. Add tomatoes, salt, tomato paste and vegetable stock. Stir until well combined. Add bay leaf, spices, salt and cilantro. Bring to a boil and immediately cover and simmer for about 40 minutes. Puree soup in a food processor or blender. Strain soup back into pot and add half and half. Stir to combine. Preheat oven to 375 degrees. Make croutons by cutting bread into 1" cubes. Place in bowl and add olive oil. Using hands mix to coat all pieces. Sprinkle with salt and pepper and place on a baking sheet in a single layer. Bake for about 6 minutes, shaking pan occasionally to insure even cooking. Bake until light golden brown. Remove and let cool. To serve, pour soup into individual bowls and float 4 croutons on top. Correct salt and pepper seasoning.

38

#  *Salads*

| | |
|---|---|
| 41 | Caesar Salad with Tuscan Croutons |
| 42 | Radicchio and Red Cabbage Citrus Salad |
| 43 | Sliced Steak Salad with Raspberry Vinaigrette |
| 44 | Pesto Chicken over Strawberry Salad |
| 45 | Seared Wasabi Sesame Tuna Salad |
| 46 | Spicy Shrimp with Citrus Vinaigrette |
| 47 | Greek Salad |
| 48 | Beet, Orange and Walnut Salad |
| 49 | Cucumber Couscous Salad |
| 50 | Chicken Salad with Almonds and Grapes |

# *Caesar Salad with Tuscan Croutons*

*Okay, so who doesn't like Caesar Salad? This one has a nice garlicky taste. The addition of the Tuscan Croutons gives this salad a lot of flavor.*

**Serves 4**

2 heads romaine
1 garlic clove crushed
2 tsp. Dijon mustard
3 Tbs. freshly squeezed lemon juice
1 egg, coddled
4 anchovy fillets, chopped
Dash of Worcestershire sauce
1/2 cup freshly grated parmesan cheese
¾ cup **Garlic Extra Virgin Olive Oil**
Freshly ground pepper
Tuscan Croutons (recipe in back of book)

Wash romaine and break into bite size pieces. Dry on paper towels. Place romaine and a piece of paper towel in a zip lock and refrigerate until use. (Towel will absorb any excess moisture). In a food processor fitted with a steel blade add garlic, mustard, lemon juice, anchovies, Worcestershire sauce, coddled egg and 2 Tbs. of the parmesan cheese. Blend until combined. Very slowly add olive oil in a steady stream to emulsify dressing. Place romaine leaves in a large salad bowl. Gently mix in dressing. Sprinkle remainder of parmesan and toss. Season with pepper and add 1 cup of Tuscan Croutons and toss again.

**Cook's Note**
To coddle egg: Place egg in a small sauce of boiling water. Make sure enough water is in pan to cover the egg. Gently add egg to water and cook 1 minute. Remove and place under cold water. Let egg sit at room temperature until use.
You may leave the anchovies out of the salad if you desire. You can replace the garlic oil with Eureka Lemon Extra Virgin Olive Oil for a more lemony than garlic flavor and in that case increase the garlic cloves to 3 and decrease the lemon juice to 2 Tbs.

# *Radicchio and Red Cabbage Citrus Salad*

*The tartness of the radicchio is pleasantly combined with the sweetness of the orange flavors. The cheese is optional but do add it for an amazing salad.*

**Serves 4-6**

---

¼ cup **Tangerine Balsamic Vinegar**
1 Tbs. minced shallots
3 Tbs**. Blood Orange Extra Virgin Olive Oil**
1 lb. red cabbage, cored, cut into thin slices
½ lb. head of Radicchio, cored, cut into thin slices
Salt and pepper to taste
½ cup dried cranberries
½ cup crumbled blue cheese

Whisk vinegar and shallots in bowl. Whisk in olive oil. Place in jar with lid in refrigerator until use. Put cabbage and radicchio in a large bowl and toss to combine. Just before serving shake jar and add enough dressing to salad to coat. Season with salt and pepper. Sprinkle salad with dried cranberries and blue cheese. Serve.

**Cook's Note**
You can use Feta cheese as a substitute but I think the saltiness of the blue cheese adds another taste note.

# Sliced Steak Salad w/ Raspberry Vinaigrette

*I love meals that can be made in less than 30 minutes. This is a great dinner salad for any time of year. Add grilled asparagus and you have a complete meal.*

Serves 4

1 1b. lean beef, boneless sirloin, flank, etc.
3 Tbs. **Raspberry Balsamic Vinegar**
2 tsp. Dijon mustard
2 Tbs. **Walnut Oil**
¼ cup **Hojiblanca Extra Virgin Olive Oil**
8 cups baby or spring salad greens (5 oz. package)
½ small red onion, sliced thin
1 ¼ cup grape tomatoes
2 oz. blue cheese or goat cheese, crumbled
¼ - ½ cup shelled walnuts

Salt and pepper steak and brush lightly with olive oil. Place in a hot skillet over medium heat and cook about 7 minutes on each side for medium rare. Remove to a plate and rest about 10 minutes. Place vinegar and mustard in bowl and whisk. Keep whisking while adding olive oil and walnut oil in a steady stream until mixture is emulsified. Add salt and pepper if desired. If you are making asparagus, add the oiled spears to a skillet and cook over medium heat for about 5 minutes, turning frequently until tender. Remove and cut into 2" pieces. Place on a plate to cool. Meanwhile, slice steak into 1/8–1/4" slices. Divide the greens between 4 plates. Top with a few slices of red onion and drizzle about 1 Tbs. dressing over salad. Divide steak slices into 4 equal portions and fan out slices on top of greens. Drizzle about another Tbs. dressing over steak and salad. Scatter cut asparagus and sprinkle salad with crumbled blue cheese and walnuts.

**Cook's Note**
If you choose to grill the steak, place oiled steak on a hot barbeque and let cook about 5 minutes each side. Oil the asparagus and add them to grill when you flip steaks over. Cook asparagus for 5 minutes.

# *Pesto Chicken over Strawberry Salad*

*Without a doubt this is one of the best tasting salads that can be used as a luncheon salad or dinner salad. The pesto recipe can be made with Basil Extra Virgin Olive Oil or you can purchase premade pesto if you have it in your pantry.*

Serves 4

4 boneless chicken breasts
½ cup pesto (recipe in back of book)
3 Tbs. **Strawberry Balsamic Vinegar**
¼ cup **Hojiblanca Extra Virgin Olive Oil**
1 ½ cups sliced ripe strawberries
1 shallot, sliced very thin
6-8 cups romaine, cut into 2" pieces
3 oz. goat cheese, crumbled

Pound chicken breasts until 1" thick. Rub completely with pesto and set aside. Put about 2 teaspoons of olive oil in skillet and cook chicken breast over medium heat about 7 minutes per side. Remove to plate and let rest for 10 minutes. Take strawberries cut off tops and slice. Place in bowl for later use. Meanwhile prepare dressing by placing balsamic in a small bowl and slowly whisking in olive oil. Place greens in large bowl and add a small amount of dressing. Divide salad onto 4 plates and sprinkle with strawberries. Place a few shallots on top. Carve chicken breasts into slices and fan out on top of greens. Pour a little more dressing over salad and top with goat cheese.

**Cook's Note**
You can use a combination of romaine lettuce and spinach which adds a slightly different taste and texture. Use shrimp in place of chicken.

# *Seared Wasabi Sesame Tuna Salad*

*Make sure you buy the freshest tuna for this recipe. The fish is seared on the outside and rare in the center. It is served over an Asian cabbage salad with a soy vinaigrette.*

Serves 4

1 – 1 ½ lbs. fresh tuna (4 tuna steaks)
Salt and pepper
1 Tbs. wasabi paste
2/3 cup sesame seeds
1-2 Tbs. **Persian Lime Extra Virgin Olive Oil**
4 cups shredded Napa cabbage
2 cups shredded red cabbage
½ raw red pepper, julienned
1 ½ cups snow peas
1/4 cup shredded carrots
4 scallions, sliced thin, white parts only
½ cup wasabi peas (optional)

**Vinaigrette:**
2 Tbs. low salt soy sauce
2 Tbs. rice vinegar
1 tsp. garlic powder
½ tsp. **Sesame Oil**
2 Tbs. **Honey Ginger Balsamic Vinegar**
1 Tbs. minced cilantro
1 Tbs. finely grated lime peel
2 Tbs. **Persian Lime Extra Virgin Olive Oil**
3 Tbs. fresh orange juice

**Wasabi Mayonnaise**
2 tsp. wasabi paste
3 Tbs. good quality mayonnaise

Salt and pepper tuna. Lightly rub tuna steaks with a little wasabi paste. Place sesame seeds on a plate and roll tuna steaks in sesame seeds until coated. Add oil to a skillet set on medium. When skillet is hot, add tuna. Cook about 2 minutes on one side, turn and repeat on other side. Remove to a plate to cool. Put cabbages in a bowl with red pepper, snow peas, and carrots and stir together. Set aside. Make vinaigrette by putting all ingredients in a jar with a lid. Close tightly and shake to incorporate all ingredients. Set aside. Make a wasabi mayonnaise by adding the two ingredients together in a small bowl and mix well. To serve, slice tuna steaks into ¼ "slices. Divide mixed salad onto 4 large dinner plates. Sprinkle with scallions and wasabi peas. Pour some vinaigrette over salad and fan out the sliced tuna on top of salad. Make a thick line of mayonnaise on the sliced tuna. Serve.

**Footnote**
If you are using the wasabi mayonnaise, place it in a squeeze bottle and squeeze a line of mayo on tuna. You can buy the wasabi paste already made and in a tube or you can make it yourself from wasabi powder which is sold in a small jar.

45

# *Spicy Shrimp with Citrus Vinaigrette*

*This salad is a quick and delicious dinner.  It is healthy and satisfying and a lovely blend of flavors.  Open a nice bottle of Riesling and share it with friends.*

**Serves 4**

1 lb. extra large shrimp, peeled and deveined
2 Tbs. **Chipotle Extra Virgin Olive Oil**
½ tsp. ground cumin
¼ cup orange juice
1 Tbs. minced shallot
1 Tbs. **Tangerine Balsamic Vinegar**
3 Tbs. **Blood Orange Extra Virgin Olive Oil**
1 Tbs. **Champagne Vinegar**
1 Tbs. orange zest
Salt and pepper to taste
6 cups Boston or butter lettuce, torn
2 mangoes sliced in ¼" slices
2 avocados sliced into ¼" slices
½ cup crumbled feta cheese
Salt and pepper to taste

Put prepared shrimp into bowl or zip lock bag.  In separate bowl add chipotle oil, cumin and 2 Tbs. orange juice and whisk to combine.   Pour over shrimp in zip lock and marinate for at least 2 hours in refrigerator.   Remove shrimp from marinade and heat skillet to medium high and add half of shrimp not crowding, cook about 2 minutes on one side.  Flip over and cook another 2 minutes.   Remove from heat and place in bowl.  Repeat with second batch of shrimp, cooking in same way.   Remove and add to other shrimp in bowl.  Set aside.  In a small bowl add shallot and vinegars and 1 Tbs. orange juice.  Slowly whisk in Blood Orange Oil and add salt and pepper to taste.  You may at this point adjust the vinaigrette to your liking, meaning, adding more vinegar if you like a tarter dressing.   Put lettuce in a large bowl and toss with the vinaigrette. Place salad equally divided onto 4 plates, place ¼ of shrimp on each and add slices of mango and avocado. Sprinkle with feta and serve.

**Cook's note**
You can replace the Tangerine Balsamic with a Honey Ginger Balsamic to add a ginger taste to recipe.

#  *Greek Salad*

*This is my typical Greek salad with the addition of the balsamic vinegar.  The lemon flavor adds a nice depth of flavor.*

**Serves 6**

2 Tbs. **Sicilian Lemon Balsamic Vinegar**
2 Tbs. red wine vinegar
1 clove garlic minced
1 tsp. dried oregano
¼ cup **Koroneiki Extra Virgin Olive Oil**
¼ cup crumbled Feta cheese
2 heads romaine lettuce
½ of an English cucumber (seedless)
½ small red onion, sliced thin
1 cup cherry tomatoes cut in half
½ cup Kalamata olives, pitted
Freshly ground pepper

In a bowl combine balsamic, red wine vinegar, garlic, and oregano. Pour olive into mixture and whisk together.  Add feta and stir.  Add salt if needed. Set aside.  Wash lettuce and cut into bite size pieces.  Lay on paper towels to dry. Put dried lettuce in a large salad bowl.  Slice cucumber into thin rounds.  Add to lettuce in bowl along with onion slices, tomatoes, and olives.  Stir in a little vinaigrette until all is coated.  Toss gently.  Sprinkle with some freshly ground pepper.  Top with extra Feta cheese if desired. Serve immediately after dressed.

**Cook's Note**
Place left over dressing in a lidded jar and keep refrigerated.  Use within 3 days. You can top the salad with grilled shrimp or chicken for a complete light meal.

# Beet, Orange and Walnut Salad

*Some salads you just can't stop eating and this is one of them. I love beets and am lucky that I can find fresh beets anytime of the year. The salad is beautiful and delicious.*

**Serves 4**

4 beets, fresh
1 Tbs. sherry vinegar
3 Tbs. **Tangerine Balsamic Vinegar**
¼ cup **Blood Orange Extra Virgin Olive Oil**
1 Tbs. **Walnut Oil**
½ medium red onion, sliced thin
6 cups arugula or baby lettuce mix
1 cup shelled walnuts, candied
1 (11 0z.) can mandarin oranges, drained
3 oz. goat cheese, crumbled (optional)

Preheat oven to 400 degrees. Wash beets to remove any sand and cut off leafy tops. Place in aluminum foil and close tightly. Bake for about 1 ½ hours or until beets are tender. Remove and let cool slightly. Peel off skin. (You might want to wear plastic gloves since beets stain your hands). Set them aside to continue cooling. Put vinegars in bowl and whisk in olive oil and walnut oil. Salt and pepper if needed. Put arugula in a large bowl and toss with walnuts and onion slices. Add enough dressing to cover slightly. Cut beets into small cubes or slices. Divide salad onto 4 plates and add scatter some orange slices, beet cubes, and a sprinkle with goat cheese.

**Cook's Note**
Pecans can be used in place of the walnuts or the nuts can be omitted. Blue cheese can be substituted for the goat cheese or if you are concerned about calories, skip the cheese.

# Cucumber Couscous Salad

*The addition of tomatoes and cucumber makes this a delightful summer salad. Try this with your kabobs or grilled meat.*

1 ½ cups instant couscous
2 cups water
¼ cup **Nocellara Extra Virgin Olive Oil**
1 tsp. grated lemon zest
1 tsp. salt
3 cups plum tomatoes, seeded and cut into ¼" dice
2 cucumbers, peeled and seeded and cut into ¼ " dice
1 Tbs. fresh lemon juice
2 Tbs. **Sicilian Lemon Balsamic Vinegar**
½ cup minced shallots
½ cup minced fresh parsley
¼ cup minced mint leaves
toasted almond slivers (optional)

Place couscous in large bowl. In a saucepan add water, 3 Tbs. olive oil, lemon zest and 1 teaspoon salt and bring to a boil. Pour liquid over couscous and stir until clumps disappear. Cover with plastic wrap and let sit 5 minutes. Meanwhile in another bowl, add tomatoes, cucumbers, lemon juice, vinegar, shallots, parsley, and mint. Drizzle with remaining 1 Tbs. olive oil and correct seasoning with salt.

**Cook's Note**
You can add toasted almond slivers to the salad just before serving. This adds a little crunch to the salad. You will need about ½ cup.

# *Chicken Salad with Almonds and Grapes*

*This salad is so refreshing. The flavors blend well together and the almonds add a nice crunch. Serve this on lettuce greens or your favorite bread.*

**Serves 6**

3 cups cooked chicken (light and dark meat)
1/3 cup minced scallions
1 ½ cup red seedless grapes (halved)
½ cup sliced toasted almonds
1 ½ cup thinly sliced celery
¾ cup good quality mayonnaise
2 Tbs. **Sicilian Lemon Balsamic Vinegar**
½ tsp. salt
Pepper to taste

Cut chicken into small cubes or shred if desired. Add to a large bowl. Mix in the scallions, grapes, almonds and celery and stir gently. In a separate small bowl whisk together the mayonnaise, balsamic vinegar and salt. Add this to chicken mixture and stir gently to fully incorporate dressing. Cool at least an hour in refrigerator. If you think dressing is too thick then add some milk to thin it. Serve cold or at room temperature.

#  *Sides*

# Potato Salad Vinaigrette

*With no mayonnaise in this potato salad, it is reminiscent of French potato salad. Serve it hot or at room temperature. It's a real crowd pleaser.*

**Serves 8**

4 lbs. red potatoes or Yukon Gold
¼ cup **Sicilian Lemon Balsamic Vinegar**
1 Tbs. cider vinegar
2 Tbs. Dijon mustard
2 garlic clove, minced
½ cup chopped scallions
1 tsp. salt
¼ cup chopped parsley
2 Tbs. chopped dill
1/3 cup **Garlic Extra Virgin Olive Oil**
salt and pepper to taste

Peel potatoes if desired. (I leave the skins on). Cut into 1" cubes. Put in a pot of boiling water and cook until tender about 15 minutes. Place in a colander and drain and immediately put them in a large bowl. Mix next 9 ingredients in a bowl. Adjust seasoning by adding salt and pepper to taste. Pour dressing over the warm potatoes. Mix gently but thoroughly. Cover bowl with plastic wrap and keep at room temperature until ready to serve.

**Cook's Note**
You can substitute Nocellara or Arbosana Extra Virgin Olive Oil for the Garlic Oil, giving the salad a nice olive taste. In that case, Increase the number of garlic cloves to 4.

# *Garlic Roasted Potatoes*

*The smell of these potatoes roasting is heavenly. They can be served with many entrées or any grilled meats.*

**Serves 6**

2 ½ lbs. small Yukon Gold or Red Skinned potatoes
½ cup **Garlic Extra Virgin Olive Oil**
3 cloves garlic minced
2 fresh sprigs of rosemary leaves, minced
2 sprigs of fresh thyme leaves, minced
1 tsp. sea salt
¼ tsp. freshly ground black pepper
2 Tbs. **Lavender Balsamic Vinegar** (optional)

Preheat oven to 400 degrees. Cut potatoes in half, if too large cut into fourths. (Leave skins on.) Place potatoes in a large bowl. Add olive oil and minced garlic. Toss. Add rosemary, thyme, salt and pepper and toss again. Place on baking pan or roasting pan and bake for about 40 minutes, until tender, turning occasionally. Before serving sprinkle with balsamic and toss.

**Cook's Note**
You can add the balsamic for an extra boost of flavor or omit it. You can also substitute Tuscan Herb Extra Virgin Olive Oil for the Garlic Extra Virgin Olive Oil.

# *Mashed Potatoes with White Truffle Oil*

*Okay, this is insanely decadent. If you happen to be a truffle nut like me, these will drive you crazy. Use as much truffle oil as you like.*

**Serves 4-6**

2 lbs. Yukon Gold potatoes, peeled
¾ cup half and half or whole milk
2 cloves garlic, grated or smashed into a paste
3 Tbs. unsalted butter
Salt to taste
**White Truffle Oil** to taste

Cut potatoes into quarters. Place in large pot and cover with cold water. Bring to a boil and reduce heat to simmer and cook uncovered for about 15 minutes until tender but not mushy. Heat half and half and garlic in a small saucepan. Bring to boil and simmer uncovered for about 10 minutes. Remove from heat and add butter. Mix until butter is dissolved. Drain potatoes and return to pot. Mash potatoes with a potato masher or fork and slowly strain milk mixture into that. Mash until combined. Season with salt and pepper to taste. You can either add the truffle oil to the potatoes or drizzle over the top of the potatoes when served. Serve immediately.

#  *Scalloped Potatoes*

*This is a wonderful rich side dish.  Serve it with grilled or roasted meats.  It also reheats well the next day.*

**Serves 6**

---

2 ½ lbs. Russet potatoes, peeled and cut into 1/8" slices
2 Tbs. **Mushroom Sage extra Virgin Olive Oil**
4 Tbs. unsalted butter
3 leeks, white and light green part, sliced thin
2 large shallots, sliced thin
3 Tbs. all purpose flour
2 cups whole milk
1 cup grated cheddar cheese
pinch of nutmeg
1 tsp. minced thyme
Salt and pepper
½ cup grated Parmesan cheese
Truffle oil (optional)

Preheat oven to 400 degrees. Place olive oil and 2 Tbs. butter in a skillet and add leeks and shallots.  Cook over medium heat for about 5 minutes.  Remove to a bowl and set aside.  Place 2 Tbs. butter in saucepan until melted. Add flour and whisk for 2 minutes.  Slowly add milk, stirring with whisk until smooth and slightly thick.  Reduce heat and stir in cheddar cheese, nutmeg and thyme.  Mixture will be thick.  Season with salt and pepper.  Butter a 9 x 13" baking dish.  Place potatoes in first, in rows, covering entire bottom of dish. Spread half of leek mixture. Add half of cheese sauce and spread over potatoes.  Repeat with another layer of potatoes followed by rest of leek mixture then cheese sauce.  Sprinkle top with Parmesan cheese. Cover baking dish with aluminum foil and bake for 35 minutes.  Remove foil and bake for another 15 minutes. Let cool slightly before serving.  Sprinkle with truffle oil.

**Cook's Note**
Every stove is different so cooking times might be longer or shorter.  To tell that it's done, look for bubbles along sides and a browning on top.  If you dare, sprinkle with truffle oil!

# *Sweet Potato Oven Fries*

*These fries are delicious.  Since they are not fried in oil they are lower in calories.  They are not crisp but are soft.  There are three variations from hot to sweet flavors. Try them all.*

Serves 4

## Chipotle Hot Sweet Potatoes

2 large sweet potatoes
1 Tbs. **Chipotle Extra Virgin Olive Oil**
2 tsp. **Garlic Extra Virgin Olive Oil**
1 tsp. salt
1/8 tsp. black pepper

## Cilantro Cinnamon Pear Sweet Potatoes

2 large sweet potatoes
1 Tbs. **Cilantro Roasted Onion Extra Virgin Olive Oil**
1 Tbs. **Cinnamon Pear Balsamic Vinegar**
1 tsp. salt
½ tsp. black pepper

## Maple Sweet Potatoes

2 large sweet potatoes
1 Tbs. **Garlic extra Virgin Olive Oil**
1 Tbs. **Maple Balsamic Vinegar**
½ tsp. ground cinnamon
1 tsp. salt
½ tsp. black pepper

Preheat oven to 425 degrees.  Cut sweet potatoes in half lengthwise.  Cut into wedges, about 4 or 5 per half. (If too long then cut in half).  Add slices to a bowl and add ingredients to them.  Mix with hands to evenly coat the sweet potatoes.  Line a baking sheet with aluminum foil and place potatoes on single layer.  You may also use a baking dish.  Bake for about 15 minutes until golden.  Loosen fries with a spatula and bake another 10 minutes.  Serve.

# Tomato and Roasted Corn Salsa

*The roasting of corn gives this salsa a nice smoky flavor. This salsa goes great as a side or just use as a dip with chips.*

**Makes 4 cups**

3 corn on cobs, husked
3 vine ripe tomatoes, seeded and diced
1 can (15 Oz.) black beans, drained
2 Tbs. fresh Lime juice
2 tsp. minced jalapeno pepper
½ cup – ¾ cup red onion, diced
1 tsp. minced garlic
½ tsp. salt
½ tsp. cumin
1 Tbs. **Persian Lime Extra Virgin Olive Oil**
1 Tbs. **Jalapeno Balsamic Vinegar**
¼ cup chopped cilantro

In a nonstick skillet add corn cobs and turn frequently until slightly browned, about 6 minutes. Remove from heat and let cool. In a large bowl add tomatoes, black beans, lime juice, jalapeno pepper, onion, garlic, salt, and cumin. Mix gently. Cut kernels off cob into the same bowl. Add olive oil and vinegar along with cilantro. Mix gently. Put in a container and cover. Refrigerate for about 1 hour before serving.

**Cook's Note**
If you don't have corn on the cob then use frozen but dry it first and add it to pan with 1 teaspoon oil. If you want to add an avocado to the salsa, you can but you must eat the salsa that day.

# *Baked Lobster Mac and Cheese*

*This recipe is so good it keeps your guests begging for more.  It is pricey to make but OMG!
well worth the effort and cost.  Serve with a salad for a nice meal.*

2 (1 ¼ to 1 ½ lb.) lobsters
5 Tbs. **Milanese Gremolata Extra Virgin Olive Oil**
1 cup chopped onion
2 garlic cloves crushed
1 bay leaf
1 Tbs. tomato paste
2 Tbs. Cognac or Brandy
3 cups water
2 Tbs. all purpose flour
1 cup heavy cream
2 cups grated Fontina cheese
2 cups grated Gruyere cheese
16 oz. small shell or gemelli pasta
2 Tbs. minced parsley
½ cup plain bread crumbs
1 tsp. **Truffle Oil** (optional)

**Cook's Note**
You may omit the truffle oil at the end or you can add more
or less. It does add another dimension to the macaroni and
cheese. Taste it first and decide for yourself.

Coat the inside of a 13 x 9 baking dish with some butter and set aside. Bring a large pot of water to boil.  Plunge lobsters headfirst and boil for about 4-5 minutes.  Remove to cutting board.  Let cool enough to handle.  Cut off claws and tails and remove meat.  Cut meat into ½ pieces and set aside.  Crack the shells and cut into 2-3 inch pieces. Heat 2 Tblsp. olive oil over medium high heat.  Add lobster body and shells and sauté about 5 minutes.  Add onion, garlic and bay leaf.  Sauté for an additional 5 minutes.  Add tomato paste, stirring for about 1 minute.  Remove from heat and add cognac.  Place back on burner and add 2 ½ cups of water.  Bring to a boil, reduce heat and cover and simmer for about 45 minutes.  Strain stock into bowl, pressing on solids to release liquid.  Discard solids and place stock in a bowl.  Set aside.  Preheat oven to 350 degrees. In a saucepan over medium heat, place 2 Tbs. of olive oil.  Add flour, stirring constantly for about one minute. Add stock and cream and stir until smooth. Simmer uncovered until sauce is reduced to 2 cups, about 8 minutes, stirring occasionally.  Add cheeses and stir until smooth. Stir in parsley.  Season with salt and pepper if necessary.  Remove from heat.  Cook pasta according to package directions. Drain and stir into cheese sauce.  Add lobster and stir carefully. Pour into prepared baking dish. In a non stick small skillet place 1 Tblsp. olive oil.  Add breadcrumbs and using a fork stir constantly until breadcrumbs begin to turn golden brown.  Place on top of casserole and bake in oven for about 20 minutes. Sprinkle truffle oil over casserole. Cool slightly before serving.

# *Roasted Spring and Summer Vegetables*

*Use a variety of fresh seasonal vegetables for roasting. Below is a list and the basic procedure. Experiment with different flavored olive oils and balsamic vinegars.*

1 lb. asparagus spears, trimmed
¼ cup **Tuscan Herb Extra Virgin Olive Oil** or
**Eureka Lemon Extra Virgin Olive Oil**
1 Tbs. **18 Year Aged Balsamic Vinegar**
Salt and pepper to taste

**Cook's Note**
Use whole baby carrots or thinly sliced carrots, zucchini slices, thinly sliced eggplant, red pepper quartered, or thickly sliced red onion rounds. Always check oven to insure vegetables are not burning. Adjust roasting time accordingly.

Preheat oven to 400 degrees. Place asparagus in a large bowl, add olive oil and balsamic and gently combine. Place on a baking sheet in a single layer. Bake for 12 to 15 minutes. Season with salt and pepper.

# *Roasted Winter Vegetables*

*There is nothing more wonderful than the smell of roasted vegetables. Serve these with winter meals.*

**Serves 6**

¼ cup **Herb de Provence Extra Virgin Olive Oil**
1½ lb. butternut squash, cubed into 1" pieces
1 large sweet potato, cubed into 1" pieces
3 Yukon gold potatoes, cubed into 1" pieces
2 parsnips, peeled, cut into 1" pieces
2 carrots, peeled, cut into 1" pieces
1 clove garlic minced
1 Tbs. minced fresh thyme
1 Tbs. minced fresh rosemary
2 Tbs. **18 Year Aged Balsamic Vinegar**

Preheat oven to 400 degrees. Place all vegetables in a large bowl. Add olive oil, vinegar, and herbs. Spread evenly on one or two baking sheets. Sprinkle with salt and pepper. Roast for 35–40 minutes, stirring every 10 to 15 minutes.

**Cook's Note**
Use Red Apple Balsamic Vinegar, Fig or Cinnamon Pear Balsamic in place of Aged Balsamic.

# Spinach Soufflé

*This is my version of a classic soufflé. It is amazing what extra virgin olive oil does for added flavor. It is a beautiful and fluffy soufflé. Remember not to open oven during cooking time.*

**Serves 4**

1 package chopped frozen spinach, defrosted (1 cup)
1 Tbs. butter
1 Tbs. Parmesan cheese
3 Tbs. **Basil Extra Virgin Olive Oil**
2 Tbs. minced shallots
3 Tbs. all purpose flour
1 tsp. salt
1/8 tsp. ground nutmeg
1/8 tsp. freshly ground black pepper
1 ½ cups whole milk
2 Tbs. **Sicilian Lemon Balsamic Vinegar**
6 eggs, separated and room temperature

Preheat oven to 400 degrees. Grease a 1 ½ to 2 quart soufflé dish with butter and sprinkle with Parmesan cheese. Bring a saucepan of lightly salted water to a boil and add spinach. Cook 2-3 minutes. Drain spinach, pushing down with a spatula to remove all juice. Let cool. Melt oil in a large saucepan and add shallots. Cook about 3-4 minutes over medium low heat. Do not burn. Stir in flour, salt, nutmeg and pepper, whisking constantly. Gradually add in milk, whisking until mixture thickens. Remove from heat. Stir in vinegar. Stir in egg yolks one at a time into milk mixture until blended. Add cooled spinach and mix to incorporate. In a bowl of an electric mixer beat egg whites until they hold stiff peaks. Fold about ¼ of egg whites into spinach mixture to make it easier to manage, and then gently fold in remainder. Pour into prepared dish and bake for 30-40 minutes until the top is well puffed and lightly browned.

# *Oven Roasted Butternut Squash*

*A favorite vegetable of mine is the butternut squash. When you roast it you bring out wonderful natural flavors. Do try this!*

2 ½ lb. butternut squash, peeled, seeded, cut into 1" cubes
3 Tbs. **Coratina Extra Virgin Olive Oil**
2 Tbs. **Red Apple Extra Virgin Olive Oil**
2 tsp. minced fresh rosemary
salt
freshly ground black pepper

Preheat oven to 400 degrees. Place squash in a large bowl and add olive oil, balsamic and rosemary. Mix and coat evenly. Spread in a single layer on a baking sheet. Sprinkle with salt and pepper. Bake for about 40 minutes until squash is slightly soft and caramelized. Serve hot.

# Glazed Carrots

*This is a favorite side.  It has a sweet taste and a beautiful presentation when baby carrots are used.*

**Serves 6**

1 lb. baby carrots or fresh carrots cut into 2" long pieces
½ cup chicken stock or chicken broth
¼ cup **Maple Balsamic Vinegar**
2 Tbs. **Butter Extra Virgin Olive Oil**
1/8 tsp. salt
1/8 tsp. freshly ground pepper

Place carrots, stock, vinegar, oil, salt and pepper in a medium skillet over medium high heat.  Bring to a boil, and then reduce heat to medium.  Cover and cook for 5 minutes.  Increase heat to high, uncover and cook an additional 5 to 6 minutes or until liquid is reduced to 3 Tbs.  Serve hot.

#  *Roasted Cauliflower*

*Serve this wonderful side vegetable with any entrée. It is delicious.*

1 (2 ½ 3 lb.) cauliflower head
¼ cup **Milanese Gremolata Extra Virgin Olive Oil**
Salt and pepper
1 garlic clove grated
1 Tbs. lemon juice
1 tsp. chopped thyme
2 Tbs. grated Parmesan Reggiano cheese (optional)

## Toasted Breadcrumbs
2 Tbs. Milanese Gremolata Extra Virgin Olive Oil
½ cup panko breadcrumbs

Preheat oven to 400 degrees. Core cauliflower and divide into large florets. Place in a large bowl with 2 Tbs. olive oil. Place on a baking sheet in single layer. (You might need 2 pans). Sprinkle lightly with salt and freshly ground pepper. Roast for 20 to 25 minutes or until tender, stirring every so often. While cauliflower is roasting make vinaigrette. In a bowl add remaining olive oil, garlic, lemon juice and thyme. Whisk together and set aside. For toasted breadcrumbs, heat olive oil in a small skillet over medium high heat. Add breadcrumbs and stir constantly until breadcrumbs are lightly browned, about 3-8 minutes. Remove cauliflower from oven, toss with vinaigrette and top with breadcrumbs and Parmesan cheese. Serve hot.

## Cook's Note
You can substitute broccoli for the cauliflower or try half cauliflower and half broccoli.

#  Yellow Rice

*This rice is a great accompaniment to any entrée with cumin. The wonderful flavors will enhance many grilled meats.*

**Serves 4**

2 tsp. **Garlic Extra Virgin Olive Oil**
2 T. minced shallots
1 ½ cup basmati or jasmine rice
2 ¼ cups low salt chicken broth
½ tsp. salt
½ tsp. turmeric
½ tsp. cumin

Heat olive oil in a medium saucepan over medium high heat. Add shallots and sauté for about 2 minutes or until soft, about 2 minutes. Add rice and cook, stirring constantly, for about 1 minute. Add broth, salt, turmeric, and cumin and stir. Bring to a boil. Reduce heat to medium low, cover and simmer for about 15 to 20 minutes or until rice is tender and liquid is absorbed. Serve hot.

**Cook's Note**
If you like hot and spicy rice then omit the Garlic Extra Virgin Olive Oil and substitute Harissa Extra Virgin Olive Oil.

#  *Entrees*

| | |
|---|---|
| 71 | Butternut Squash and Chicken Risotto |
| 72 | Roasted Vegetable Lasagna |
| 73 | Pasta with Corn Sauce and Arugula Pesto |
| 74 | Shrimp Scampi Pasta |
| 75 | Broccoli Rabe and Sausage Pasta |
| 77 | Pork Tenderloin with Blueberry Sauce |
| 78 | Bruschetta over Breaded Pork Cutlets |
| 60 | Stuffed Poblano Peppers |
| 81 | Filet Mignon with Black Cherry Cabernet Sauce |
| 82 | Meatloaf |
| 83 | Beef Short Ribs over Blue Cheese Polenta |
| 85 | Seafood Paella |
| 86 | Baked Fish with Tomatoes and Potatoes |
| 87 | Fish Tacos with Slaw and Curried Mayo |

#  *Entrees*

# *Butternut Squash and Chicken Risotto*

*I love risotto, I mean LOVE risotto. This is an all in one satisfying entrée. All you need is a salad as a side dish and you have a complete meal.*

**Serves 6**

1 large boneless chicken breast, skinless
3 Tbs. **Milanese Gremolata Extra Virgin Olive Oil**
¼ cup bread crumbs
1 Tbs. minced parsley
¼ cup Parmesan cheese
1 small butternut squash (about 1 lb.)
5 cups low salt chicken broth
3 cups water
2 fresh sage leaves
½ tsp. saffron threads
2 Tbs. butter
2 oz. pancetta or bacon, diced
½ cup minced shallots
2 cups Arborio rice
½ cup dry white wine
1 cup grated parmesan
1 tsp. truffle oil (optional)

### Cook's Note
You can substitute Pumpkin or Sweet Potato for the Butternut Squash or you can omit the chicken from this recipe. All in all, you have a great tasting risotto.

Preheat oven to 400 degrees. Cut chicken breast in half. Rub chicken breasts with 1 Tbs. olive oil and set aside. In a bowl mix bread crumbs, parsley and cheese. Dip chicken breasts in dry mixture and place in a shallow baking dish. Meanwhile prepare squash. Peel squash, remove seeds and cut into ½" cubes. Place in bowl and toss with 1 Tbs. olive oil and a slight sprinkling of salt. Place on baking sheet. Put baking sheet in oven on one shelf and chicken in baking dish on another shelf. Bake for about 30 minutes stirring squash once. Remove both from oven and let rest. Cut chicken into 1" pieces. Put broth, water, sage leaves and saffron in a large saucepan, cover and simmer. In large pot or skillet put butter and remaining 1 Tbs. olive oil on medium heat and add pancetta. Cook until lightly browned. Remove with slotted spoon to a small bowl. In same pot where pancetta was cooked, put shallots and cook until translucent and soft. Add rice and stir to coat. Add wine and stir until evaporated. Slowly ladle about 1 ½ cups of stock into rice, stirring often. Cover and simmer 5 minutes or until rice has absorbed stock. Repeat this process in same way stirring every few minutes. If rice gets dry, add stock. Continue until last ladle of stock is left. Mix in squash, add last ladle of stock and stir. Rice should be a little al dente but creamy. Add chicken cubes, stir and add Parmesan stirring to incorporate. Stir in truffle oil. Serve.

# Roasted Vegetable Lasagna

*When you just want a great meatless meal, this lasagna fits the bill. It is tasty and filled with roasted vegetables. All you will need is a crusty piece of bread and a glass of wine.*

**Serves 8**

2 Tbs. **Tuscan Herb Extra Virgin Olive Oil**
1 cup chopped onions
2 garlic cloves, minced
1 (28 oz.) can crushed tomatoes in puree
3 Tbs. tomato paste
1 bay leaf 3 large basil leaves
1 tsp. salt
1/8 tsp. freshly ground black pepper
3 zucchini, cut in ¼" slices
1 large eggplant cut in ¼" slices
3 Tbs. **Garlic Extra Virgin Olive Oil**
3 Portobello mushrooms, cut in ¼" slices
1 lb. lasagna boxed lasagna noodles
15 oz. container ricotta cheese
4 oz. creamy goat cheese, room temperature
¼ cup pesto
1 cup grated Parmesan cheese
1 egg, slightly beaten
1 (12 oz.) jar roasted red peppers
6 sundried tomatoes julienned
½ cup grated mozzarella

Preheat oven to 400 degrees. Heat 2 Tblsp. Tuscan Herb olive oil in heavy saucepan, add onion and cook over medium low heat for 5 minutes until onions are translucent. Add garlic and cook another minute. Add tomatoes and bay leaf along with basil leaves, stir and cook uncovered for about 45 minutes, stirring occasionally. Place zucchini and eggplant in a large bowl and add 2-3 Tblsp. garlic olive oil and coat well. Place on baking pans in single layer. Bake for 15 minutes then turn vegetables over and cook another 10 minutes. Remove and place on a platter. Place sliced mushrooms on baking sheet and sprinkle with olive oil. Bake for 10 minutes. Remove to a platter. Put a large pot of salted water on stovetop and bring to a boil. Add lasagna noodles 2 at a time and continue until all noodles are submerged. Stir lightly to avoid sticking. Cook until al dente, about 8 minutes. Remove and place in strainer under cold water to stop the cooking. Layer noodles between wax paper until using. In a medium bowl combine ricotta, goat cheese, pesto, ½ cup Parmesan cheese, and the egg. Mix until incorporated. Remove bay leaf and basil leaves from tomato mixture. Place a layer of noodles covering bottom of a 9 x 13" non stick or glass baking pan. Spread ½ of eggplant slices, ½ of zucchini slices, ½ of mushrooms, ½ of roasted peppers and ½ of sundried tomatoes on top of noodles. Spread ½ of the ricotta mixture on top. Place another layer of noodles on top, then 1 ¼ cups tomato mixture, followed by all of vegetables. Place one more layer of noodles, followed by 1 ¼ cups sauce topped with the rest of ricotta. Sprinkle ½ cup of Parmesan and ½ cup of mozzarella. Bake for 40 minutes. If cheese begins to brown too quickly, cover pan with foil. Remove from oven and let cool 10 minutes before serving.

# *Pasta with Corn Sauce and Arugula Pesto*

*I had a version of this recipe in a restaurant. My recipe is easier and less time consuming. It is a great, light, summer pasta using fresh summer vegetables. The flavors are sublime.*

**Serves 6**

2 cups arugula leaves
1/3 cup shelled pistachio nuts
1 garlic clove, crushed
1/8 tsp. red pepper flakes
½ cup **Milanese Gremolata Extra Virgin Olive Oil**
Salt to taste
3 sweet corn on cobs
2 Tbs. unsalted butter
1 cup chopped onion
¼ cup white wine
2 cups chicken broth
1 bay leaf
1 1b. fettuccine pasta
1 cup halved sweet grape or cherry tomatoes

**Cook's Note**
You can substitute vegetable broth for the chicken broth to keep this dish totally vegetarian. For a nice entrée finish the dish by adding grilled scallops or shrimp on top of the pasta.

Wash and dry the arugula. Lightly toast pistachio nuts. Place nuts in food processor with a steel blade and pulse a few times. Rough chop arugula and add to processor along with garlic, red pepper and olive oil. Pulse until smooth. Taste and correct with salt. Place in an airtight container and refrigerate until use. Serve at room temperature. Add water to a large saucepan and bring to a boil. Submerge corn on cobs for 3 minutes. Remove cobs and immediately place under cold water. Cut kernels off cobs, reserving cobs. Put butter in saucepan and add onion. Sauté until translucent about 3-5 minutes, stirring occasionally. Add wine, broth and bay leaf. Bring to boil and add cobs. Reduce heat and simmer uncovered for 30 minutes. Remove bay leaf and cobs. Strain stock, reserving liquid. Press down on onions to release all liquid. Place liquid with i/2 of corn kernels in food processor and puree until smooth. Add 2 Tblsp. Heavy cream and pulse. Remove sauce and set aside. Prepare pasta according to directions. To serve, reheat sauce and toss corn sauce with pasta. Place on center of plate and spoon some corn kernels over pasta followed by about 2-3 Tbs. of Pesto Sauce. Scatter a few tomato halves. A little freshly ground pepper will finish the dish.

# *Shrimp Scampi Pasta*

*If you enjoy shrimp scampi this recipe will send you over the top. It is full of garlicky flavor and after that first mouthful…… well, see for yourself!*

Serves 4

1 lb. extra large shrimp, peeled and deveined
¾ lb. to 1 lb. angel hair pasta
1 tsp. salt
4 Tbs. **Garlic Extra Virgin Olive Oil**
3 Tbs. unsalted butter
4 garlic cloves, grated or minced
½ tsp. red pepper flakes
½ cup dry white wine
1 Tbs. fresh lemon juice
1 tsp. lemon zest
½ cup chopped parsley
½ cup grated parmesan cheese

Rinse and pat dry shrimp. Put a large pot of water on high heat, add salt and bring to a boil. In a large skillet over medium heat add 2 Tbs. olive oil and 2Tbs. butter. Add garlic, crushed red pepper and shrimp and cook for about 2 minutes until shrimp are pink. Remove shrimp and set aside. Turn heat to medium high and add wine and lemon juice to pan, whisking until reduced by half. Add 2 more Tbs. olive oil and 1 Tbs. butter, turn down heat and add shrimp back to skillet. Toss in parsley and lemon zest and mix. Remove from heat. In the pot of boiling water add pasta and cook according to directions until al dente. Drain pasta. Add pasta to skillet with shrimps and sauce. To serve drizzle a little more oil on top of pasta and top with grated cheese.

**Cook's Note**
You can use Milanese Gremolata Extra Virgin Olive Oil or Eureka Lemon Extra Virgin Olive Oil in place of the Garlic Extra Virgin Olive Oil. In both cases add 2 more garlic cloves for a total of 6. If you don't want to use wine you can make your own shrimp stock by placing shrimp shells in 2 cups water with ½ cup chopped onion. Boil then simmer for about 20 to 30 minutes. Use ½ cup.

**Footnote**
If you don't want to use butter replace it with 2 Tbs. Butter Olive Oil.

74

# *Broccoli Rabe and Sausage Pasta*

*This is another favorite of mine. I love the tartness of the broccoli rabe with the sweet and hot sausage. Yum!*

**Serves 4 as an entrée or 6 as first course**

2 tsp. sea salt
1 ½ to 2 lbs. broccoli rabe
1/3 cup **Tuscan Herb Extra Virgin Olive Oil**
½ lb. Italian sweet sausage
½ lb. Italian hot sausage
6 garlic cloves thinly sliced
Pinch red pepper flakes
¾ cup low salt chicken broth
8 oz. penne rigatoni (or any medium size pasta)
¼ cup toasted pine nuts
½ cup Parmigiano- Reggiano cheese plus extra

**Cook's Note**
Substitute the Tuscan Herb Extra Virgin Olive Oil with Garlic Extra Virgin Olive Oil. In that case, reduce the garlic cloves to 3 instead of 6.

Bring a large pot of water to a boil and add salt. Cut stems off broccoli rabe. (Hold bunch together and just cut straight across bottom, cutting most of stems off). Add broccoli rabe to boiling water and cook about 2 to 3 minutes. Remove with slotted spoon, leaving water behind in pot. Put broccoli in colander to drain and pour cold water over it to stop the cooking. Squeeze gently to remove any excess water. Place on cutting board and rough chop it. Set aside. In a skillet over medium heat add olive oil. Remove sausage meat from casings and add to skillet along with garlic and red pepper, stirring and breaking up sausage meat with a wooden spoon. Brown the sausage for about 5 to 7 minutes. Add broccoli rabe and chicken broth and lower heat, stirring all ingredients until heated through. Season with salt if needed. Put pasta in pot which has broccoli rabe water, bring to boil and cook according to directions on box. When done, remove pasta to a colander to drain, reserving a ladle full or two of pasta water. Mix pasta into sausage mixture in skillet and add some of the pasta water if needed. Stir in cheese. Check for seasoning. Add salt if needed and another Tbs. of olive oil. Mix well. Sprinkle with pine nuts. Place in bowls and pass around extra cheese.

Pork Tenderloin with Blueberry Balsamic Sauce

# *Pork Tenderloin with Blueberry Balsamic Sauce*

*This dish can be made under an hour. This is a wonderful sauce and can be used for seared duck as well as chicken. Freeze the leftover sauce for other uses.*

Serves 4

1 ½ to 2 lbs. pork tenderloin
2 Tbs. **Milanese Gremolata Extra Virgin Olive Oil**
3 Tbs. minced shallots
2 garlic cloves, minced
¼ cup port wine
½ cup **Blueberry Balsamic Vinegar**
¼ cup low salt chicken broth
2 sprigs fresh thyme
1 cup fresh blueberries

Trim silver skin off tenderloin. Dry the pork with paper towels. Salt and pepper the tenderloin. Heat olive oil in skillet over medium high heat. Add tenderloin and lightly brown on all sides for about 2 minutes each side. Preheat oven to 400 degrees. Place tenderloin on rimmed baking sheet or baking dish and cook in oven for 10 – 12 minutes or until internal temperature reads 145 degrees. Remove from oven and place on plate and tent with aluminum foil. Let rest. Place shallots in skillet which you have browned meat. Add a little more olive oil if needed. Cook for a few minutes until soft. Add garlic and cook for another 2 minutes. Deglaze pan with port, scraping up bits while stirring. Cook until port is almost absorbed. Add balsamic and simmer until reduced by half. Add chicken broth, thyme, and blueberries. Bring to a boil, and then turn heat to medium. Cook until sauce thickens and blueberries burst slightly. Add any pan juices from resting tenderloin to sauce pot. Stir. Slice tenderloin into ½" slices. Fan out on individual plate and pour sauce over. Decorate with a sprig of thyme.

**Cook's Note**
This is an easy dish to prepare. If there is leftover sauce it can be refrigerated or frozen. It is possible to omit the port wine but you will lose some depth of flavor.

77

# *Bruschetta over Breaded Pork Cutlets*

*This is a wonderful light and refreshing dinner which is sure to impress. It can be ready in one hour. Use only ripe tomatoes in season. The smoky mozzarella sends this dish over the top.*

4 pork cutlets or boneless pork cutlets
4 ripe tomatoes
¼ cup fresh basil, julienne
1 clove garlic, minced
2 Tbs. **18 Year Aged Balsamic Vinegar**
¼ cup + 2 Tbs. **Nocellara Extra Virgin Olive Oil**
½ cup bread crumbs
1 egg
4 oz. smoked mozzarella

**Cook's Note**
Nocellara can be replaced with any good quality Sicilian Extra Virgin Olive Oil. The pork cutlets can be replaced with veal cutlets or chicken cutlets. Cooking times might vary depending on thickness of cutlets. If bruschetta was placed in refrigerator; bring to room temperature before serving.

Place pork cutlets between 2 pieces of wax paper and pound with the flat side of a meat tenderizer. Cutlets should be 1/8" thick. Remove from paper and set cutlets aside. Cut tomatoes in half then cut halves into eight slices for a total of 16 slices per tomato. Put in a large bowl and add julienned basil and minced garlic. Add balsamic vinegar and 3 Tbs. of olive oil. Mix well. Place in refrigerator or leave at room temperature for 1 hour. Mix egg and 2 Tbs. water in a bowl. Set aside. Spread breadcrumbs on a plate. Put 3 Tbs. olive oil in non stick skillet. Dip cutlets in egg then in breadcrumbs. Lay cutlets in skillet but do not crowd. Cook over medium heat about 3 minutes on one side, turn and cook another 3 on the other. Cutlets should be golden brown. (Add more oil if needed). Drain cutlets on paper towels. Remove cutlets to a baking sheet. Set oven to broil. Cut smoked mozzarella into thin slices and lay on top of cutlet. Place under broiler for one minute or until cheese is melted. Check carefully that cheese is not burning. Remove from broiler and place cutlet on individual plate. Spoon ¼ of bruschetta on top. Make sure to spoon sauce with it. Serve.

**Footnote:** For an impressive plate, drizzle balsamic glaze (in back of book) on plate in a soft zigzag pattern then lay cutlets topped with bruschetta. You will have to reduce the balsamic in the bruschetta to only 1 Tbs.

# *Stuffed Poblano Peppers*

*These peppers are spicy hot. They can be made rather quickly. You can use many different kinds of chicken sausage, beef or pork.*

**Serves 4**

4 poblano chilies
2 Tbs. **Garlic Extra Virgin Olive Oil**
1 ¼ cup chopped onion
2 cloves garlic, minced
1 (14 oz) can diced tomatoes
2 Tbs. **Aged Balsamic Vinegar**
½ tsp. salt
1/8 tsp. freshly ground pepper
1 Tbs. oregano
½ tsp. ground cumin
chicken sausage (about 1 ¼ lb. to 1 ½ lb.)
1 ¾ cup shredded Monterey Jack cheese

**Cook's Note**
If you like more sauce you can double the recipe.

Preheat oven to 350 degrees. Place peppers on open flame of gas stove, turning each side, until fully charred. Watch carefully when doing this. If you don't have a gas stove you can place chilies on rack under broiler. Turn constantly until blistered about 4-6 minutes. Transfer chilies to a plastic or paper bag and close to allow chilies to steam for about 5-8 minutes. Run skins off chilies with a paper towel, or knife. If you have sensitive skin, try using gloves when removing skins. Wash hands thoroughly after. Place 1 Tbs. olive oil in a heated saucepan and add onion and cook 5 minutes. Add garlic and cook another 2 minutes. Add to that the tomatoes, balsamic, salt, pepper, oregano and cumin. Bring to a boil then lower heat and simmer uncovered for about 10 minutes. Puree sauce in blender or food processor. Remove skins from sausages. Place 1 Tbs. olive oil in a skillet and add sausage meat, breaking it up with a wooden spoon to insure even cooking. Cook until light brown. Take chilies and make a slit from top to bottom. Remove seeds. Stir ½ of tomato mixture into sausage meat and add in ¾ cup of cheese. Stir until cheese is melted. Place stuffed chilies into a 13 X 9 baking dish and top each chili pepper opening with some cheese. Spoon rest of sauce around peppers. Bake in oven for 30 minutes.

# *Filet Mignon w/ Black Cherry Cabernet Sauce*

*When you want something elegant and simple to make, this is it. This is a simply delicious sauce. Serve truffle mash potatoes and green beans for a beautiful presentation.*

**Serves 4**

2 Tbs. unsalted butter
2 Tbs. **Wild Mushroom and Sage Extra Virgin Olive Oil**
4 filet mignon steaks (about 4-5 oz. each, 2" thick)
1/3 cup chopped shallots
1 cup good quality Cabernet Sauvignon
¼ cup **Black Cherry Balsamic Vinegar**
2/3 cup beef stock or broth
1 garlic clove, crushed
2 fresh rosemary sprigs about 3-4" in length plus more for decoration
Salt and pepper if needed
(truffle sea salt optional)

**Cook's Note**
You may use truffled salt for preparing the steaks for cooking. Always allow steaks to get to room temperature before adding them to a hot skillet. This prevents sticking to the pan. Test the steaks for doneness using a meat thermometer. For rare temperature should be 120 degrees, medium rare is 125 degrees, and medium is 130 degrees. If using thinner filets be sure to cut cooking time.

Preheat oven to 400 degrees. Melt 1 Tbs. butter and 1 Tbs. olive oil in skillet over medium high heat. Sprinkle both sides of steaks lightly with salt and pepper. (You can use truffled sea salt for this). Place steaks in skillet and cook for 2-3 minutes, turn and cook another 3 minutes. Remove steaks from skillet and place on a baking sheet. Cook in oven for 5 minutes. In the same skillet as steaks were in, add 1 Tbs. olive oil along with shallots and sauté for I minute. Stir in vinegar and boil for 2 minutes, allowing vinegar to evaporate a little. Test steaks in oven for desired doneness. (Do not over cook these.). Remove steaks from oven to a plate and let sit on counter for 5-10 minutes. Meanwhile, add wine, broth, garlic and rosemary sprigs to sauce in skillet. Bring to a boil. Cook uncovered for about 8 to 10 minutes or until reduced to ¾ cup. Strain sauce, add in any juices from resting filet and whisk in 1 Tbs. butter. To serve, put some sauce on plate and place steak on top. Add a small sprig of rosemary across top of steak.

# *Meatloaf*

*This is a great comfort food dish for the family. Serve this entrée with mashed potatoes and a green vegetable. It is a moist meatloaf that makes great leftovers for sandwiches.*

**Serves 4**

1 Tbs. **Tuscan Herb Extra Virgin Olive Oil**
¾ cup minced onion
1 ½ tsp. salt
1 ½ tsp. freshly ground black pepper
2 lbs. (total) ground beef, pork, turkey combo (or all beef)
1 Tbs. garlic powder
¾ cup Italian flavored bread crumbs
1 egg, slightly beaten
1 tsp. Worcestershire sauce
2 Tbs. minced fresh parsley
5 Tbs. **18 Year Aged Balsamic Vinegar**
1 (15 oz.) can tomato sauce
¼ cup milk

Preheat oven to 350 degrees. Put olive oil in skillet and cook onions until translucent and tender. Remove from heat and season with salt and pepper. Set aside. In a large bowl add ground meats, onions, garlic powder, bread crumbs, egg, Worcestershire sauce, parsley and 2 Tbs. of vinegar. Add to this, ½ can of tomato sauce. Slowly add milk 1 Tblsp. at a time as needed to keep meatloaf moist but not soggy. Mold into a 5" x 9" loaf pan. Bake for 40 minutes. Increase oven to 400 degrees and bake for another 15 minutes. The internal temperature of the meatloaf should be around 160 degrees. In a small bowl mix the rest of the tomato sauce with the remaining 3 Tbs. of balsamic vinegar. Pour this over the meatloaf and continue baking another 10 minutes. Serve hot.

**Cook's Note**
This recipe is easily doubled for more servings, a good reason to buy more loaf pans.

# Beef Short Ribs over Blue Cheese Polenta

*The addition of the Balsamic Vinegar brings out the beefy flavor in these tasty short ribs. Buy the meatiest ribs, marbleized with some fat. This recipe requires effort and time, but worth it.*

**Serves 8**

5 lbs. beef short ribs, with bone, cut into 4" pieces
2 Tbs. Emeril's Original Essence dry rub
1 Tbs. flour
1 medium onion, peeled and quartered
2 celery stalks, cut into 1" pieces
3 carrots, peeled, cut into 1" pieces
8 large cloves garlic minced
2 Tbs. tomato paste
½ cup **18 year Aged Balsamic Vinegar**
2 cups red wine, Cabernet Sauvignon or Zinfandel
4 cups beef stock or beef broth
2 4" stems fresh rosemary
4 sprigs fresh thyme
2 bay leaves
3 Tbs. minced parsley for garnish

**Blue Cheese Polenta**

3 cups water
3 cups milk
1 ½ cups polenta
4 oz. blue cheese, crumbled

**Cook's Note**

Short Rib stew can be made the day before. Place in refrigerator overnight and spoon fat off top before serving. Reheat in a 350 degree oven for about 1 hour or until heated through.

Preheat oven to 450. Place dry rub and flour in large zip lock bag and add 5 pieces of beef. Shake to cover lightly. Set aside on dish and continue until all pieces are coated in same way. Place meat in a large roasting pan and put in oven. Roast for 30 minutes. Remove from oven, put meat on platter and drain fat. Add onion, celery and carrots to pan and return to oven for 15 minutes. Remove from oven to stovetop and add garlic and tomato paste and stir, not allowing tomato paste to burn. Add balsamic and ½ cup wine to deglaze pan. Stir constantly to incorporate. Add rest of wine and beef stock along with herbs. Lower oven to 350 degrees. Return meat to roasting pan. (Make sure meat is covered with liquid, if not, add water to cover them.) Cover the pan and let roast in oven for 4 hours. Remove from oven. Remove meat and keep warm. Remove bones and discard. Take liquid and vegetables from pan and strain into a pot, pushing down on solids. Put on medium heat and reduce liquids until it becomes thicker like gravy. While it is reducing, make polenta. Heat water and milk in saucepan and bring to simmer, but do not boil. Whisk in polenta a little at a time, stirring as you go. Cover and simmer for 15 minutes, stirring every so often. If too thick add more water. Remove from heat and stir in blue cheese. To serve, place some polenta on each plate, top with short ribs, pour some gravy over ribs and finish with a sprinkling of parsley.

#  Seafood Paella

*If you like seafood and spices you'll enjoy this version of paella. Always buy fresh seafood.*
*Don't forget some crusty bread to soak up the sauce.*

**Serves 6**

---

1 whole 3 lb. chicken, cut into 10 pieces
¼ cup **Harissa Extra Virgin Olive Oil**
3 (4") Spanish chorizo sausages
1 large yellow onion, diced
3 cloves garlic, crushed
½ red pepper, seeded, diced
2 cups low salt chicken broth
2 cups fish stock or clam juice
Pinch of saffron threads
1 ½ cups Arborio rice
1 (14.5 oz.) can whole tomatoes, drained and crushed
¼ cup fresh cilantro chopped
½ tsp. turmeric
½ tsp. ground cumin
1 tsp. dried oregano leaves
1 Tbs. sweet paprika
1 dozen little neck clams, scrubbed
2 dozen mussels, scrubbed
Zest of 1 lemon
1 1b. extra large shrimp, peeled
12 sea scallops

**Cook's Note**
Use boneless, skinless chicken thighs to save on fat. You will need 2 ½ lbs.

Heat oil over medium heat in a large skillet or sauté pan Add chicken and cook until all sides are browned, about 10 minutes. Remove chicken to a large bowl. Loosen bits from bottom of pan with wooden spoon. Slice sausage into ¼" rounds. Add sausage to pan and brown lightly. Remove sausage and place in bowl with chicken and set aside. Place onions, garlic and red pepper in the same pan and cook until soft, about 10 minutes. Heat broth and fish stock in a saucepan and add saffron. Stir rice into onion mixture in sauté pan. Cook for 1 minute. Add tomatoes and cilantro and cook another minute. Add broth from saucepan along with turmeric, cumin, oregano, and paprika. Cover and simmer about 10-15 minutes. Add clams, mussels, and lemon zest. Add to this, chicken pieces and chorizo and cook for another 10 minutes. Add shrimp and scallops and cook another 10 minutes. Stir occasionally. Make sure all shells are opened. Serve in large individual bowls. Sprinkle with some cilantro.

**Footnote:**
To rid clams and mussels of sand prior to cooking, place them in a large bowl and fill with cold water. Stir in ½ cup cornmeal and 1 cup salt. Cover pot with aluminum foil and place in refrigerator for 2 hours. When ready, rinse several times.

85

# *Baked Fish with Tomatoes and Potatoes*

*This dish is based on an Old Italian recipe. The fish has such an incredible taste and is sure to please. This is a great one pan meal.*

2 lbs. firm white fish fillets, such as red snapper, grouper
1 ½ lb. Yukon gold potatoes, peeled and sliced 1/8" thick
¼ cup **Milanese Gremolata Extra Virgin Olive Oil**
1 Tbs. chopped parsley
1 Tbs. chopped oregano or thyme
3 cloves garlic, sliced
1 teaspoon salt
Fresh black pepper
3-4 plum tomatoes, sliced into ¼" pieces
2 Tbs. capers
1 Tbs. grated lemon zest
¼ cup plain breadcrumbs

Preheat oven to 400 degrees. In a bowl add potato slices, 3 Tbs. olive oil, parsley, oregano and garlic slices, salt and pepper. Toss together. Spread potatoes in a 13 x 9 x 2-inch glass baking or casserole dish   Bake for 15 minutes. Remove from oven and top potatoes with a layer of tomatoes. Lightly salt and pepper fish and lay on top of tomatoes. Sprinkle capers and lemon zest. Sprinkle the breadcrumbs over top and drizzle with the last Tblsp. of olive oil. Return the pan to the oven and bake another 15 minutes. Remove and let sit about 5 minutes before serving.

**Cook's Note**
You can also substitute with striped bass.

# *Fish Tacos with Slaw and Curried Mayo*

*This dish can be made with several variations. It can be placed on a brioche roll or a hamburger roll instead of a soft tortilla or it can be placed on a ciabatta roll. The fish can be grilled or sautéed instead of frying to save a few calories. Consider 2 tacos per serving.*

**Serves 4**

1 ½ lbs. cod, striped bass or tilapia
Vegetable oil for frying
1 pkg. Beer Batter mix, follow directions
½ head red cabbage finely shredded
½ head green cabbage finely shredded
1 red pepper, julienned
½ cup minced scallions
2 tsp. sugar
2 Tbs. fresh lime juice
2 Tbs. rice wine vinegar
1 tsp. **Sesame Seed Oil**
3 ripe tomatoes, peeled, seeded and diced
8 flour tortillas

## Curried Mayo
2 tsp. **Harissa Extra Virgin Olive Oil**
1 cup good quality mayonnaise
1/8 tsp. cayenne pepper
1 Tbs. curry powder
1 tsp. cumin
2 tsp. garlic powder
2 tsp. **Honey Ginger Balsamic Vinegar**
2 Tbs. minced fresh cilantro leaves
Salt to taste

## Cook's Note
If making a sandwich in place of the taco, slice the tomatoes instead of dicing, top fish with slaw and sliced tomatoes and add a leaf or two of romaine lettuce followed by curried mayo.

Dry the fish with paper towels. Cut fish into 1" bite size pieces. Place enough vegetable oil in large pot and bring to temperature for frying. Follow directions on batter package for fish. When fish is cooked, place on paper towels to absorb any grease. Place in a large serving bowl. To make slaw, place cabbages, red pepper, scallions and sugar in a large bowl and mix gently. In a separate bowl mix lime juice, vinegar and sesame oil together. Add to cabbages and toss gently. Put tomatoes in another serving bowl. To make curried mayo place olive oil, mayonnaise, pepper, curry powder, cumin, garlic powder, vinegar and cilantro in a food processor on medium speed until blended. Place mayo in serving bowl. To serve, heat tortillas in a heated non stick skillet and cook each one about 15-20 seconds on one side, turn and cook 15-20 seconds on other side. Stack on a plate and cover with a tea towel to keep warm. Place all serving bowls on table and allow guests to build their own taco. Start with fish, then slaw followed by tomatoes and finish with mayo on top.

## Footnote
As an alternative to frying the fish, salt and pepper the fish and place ¼ cup unsalted butter in a skillet and cook about 2-3 minutes on each side. Use more butter if needed. Continue with rest of recipe.

You can also heat tortilla in a 350 degree oven for about 1-2 minutes until heated and soft, then cover with foil until ready to serve.

# Scallops in Tarragon Sauce over Spinach

*The unexpected tarragon flavor over the briny scallops is a great combination. Top with the Toasted breadcrumbs for a little crunch.*

1 Tbs. + 2 tsp. **Tarragon Extra Virgin Olive Oil**
2 T. butter
½ cup minced shallots
½ cup dry white wine
½ cup clam juice
2/3 cup heavy cream
2 Tbs. chopped fresh tarragon
1 Tbs. Pernod or other Anise flavored liqueur
16 large sea scallops
6 cups baby spinach

**Gremolata Breadcrumbs**
2 Tbs. **Milanese Gremolata Extra Virgin Olive Oil**
½ cup panko breadcrumbs
Salt and pepper to taste

**Cook's Note**
You can also substitute the Milanese Gremolata Olive Oil for the Tarragon Olive Oil in the recipe for a more lemony garlic flavor.

Melt 1 Tbs. olive oil with 1 Tbs. butter in a skillet over medium heat. Add shallots and sauté 3 minutes. Add wine and boil, reducing by half, about 2 minutes. Add clam juice and boil 1 minute. Reduce heat and add cream, 1 Tbs. tarragon and Pernod. Simmer until sauce coats back of spoon, about 2 minutes. Season with salt and pepper. Keep warm. Melt 1 Tbs. butter with the 2 tsp. Olive oil in a large non tick skillet over medium heat. Dry scallops and sprinkle with salt and pepper. Cook 8 scallops at a time until lightly browned and almost cooked through, about 2 minutes per side. Do not overcrowd scallops when cooking. Repeat with the second batch. Transfer scallops to platter sand set aside. Add spinach to drippings in skillet and toss until it begins to wilt, about 2 minutes. Remove from heat. To serve spoon sauce on plate, divide spinach and place on plate, top with 4 scallops each and a little more sauce and finish with chopped tarragon or gremolata breadcrumbs.

To make breadcrumbs: Heat oil in skillet over medium high heat. Add breadcrumbs. Stir constantly until lightly browned, about 2 minutes. Taste and add salt and pepper if needed.

# *Salmon with Orange Champagne Glaze*

*This has a lovely orange flavor.  The salmon can be seared and baked or grilled.*
*Serve this on a yellow rice or cumin seasoned rice to meld flavors.*

4 (6 oz.) pieces salmon fillets with skin
2 Tbs. **Blood Orange Extra Virgin Olive Oil**
1 Tbs.  finely chopped rosemary
2 cloves garlic, minced
½ teaspoon salt
1/8 teaspoon black pepper
1 cup **Orange Champagne Balsamic Glaze**

Put 1 Tbs. olive oil and rosemary, garlic. Salt, pepper, and glaze in a bowl and whisk to combine.  Score skin of salmon by making 3 diagonal cuts about 1 inch apart and about ¼ inch into skin.  Make 3 cuts the other way over first cuts creating a diamond pattern.  Put glaze and salmon into a zip lock bag and place in refrigerator for 1 hour.  Preheat oven to 325 degrees.  Remove salmon from refrigerator, discarding marinade.  Place 1 Tbs. olive oil in skillet on medium heat.  Add salmon to skillet skin side and cook about 4 minutes on each side.  Place on baking sheet and put in oven to cook for another 10-15 minutes until done.  Remove from oven and let rest 5-10 minutes before serving.

**Cook's Note**
To grill salmon on barbecue, turn grill to medium high, oil grates, remove salmon from marinade and place on grill discarding rest of marinade.  Cook for about 5-6 minutes and turn over.  Let rest for about 10 minutes before serving.

# Bass with Ginger Sesame Sauce

*This is my favorite go to fish recipe. You might make it your own. It is based on the recipe from Eric Ripert, chef and restaurateur.*

4 bass fish filets (about 5-6 oz. each)
dash of Old Bay Seasoning
1 Tbs. minced shallots
3 Tbs. **Honey Ginger Balsamic Vinegar**
3 Tbs. low salt soy sauce
2 Tbs. water
2 Tbs. **Sesame Seed Oil**
1 Tbs. oyster sauce
1 Tbs. **Cobrancosa Extra Virgin Olive Oil**
1 lb. bok choy
2 Tbs. butter
2 Tbs. toasted sesame seeds

**Cook's Note**
You may substitute bass with basa, Chilean sea bass, red snapper, mahi mahi, or black cod.

Wash fish and dry with paper towels. Salt and Pepper fish and lightly sprinkle with Old Bay seasoning. Set aside. Place shallots, vinegar, soy sauce, water, sesame oil, and oyster sauce in a bowl and whisk together. Cut bok choy into 4" pieces. (If using baby bok choy cut 1" off bottom and pull stalks apart.) Fill a large pot with water, bring to a boil and add bok choy. Cook about 3 minutes. Remove and drain, reserving about 2 Tblsp. of broth. Stop the cooking by submerging bok choy under cold water. Set aside. Put olive oil in skillet on medium heat. Add fish filets and cook about 6 minutes on one side, turn and cook another 6 minutes. Add more olive oil if needed. Meanwhile place ½" of water in another skillet and bring to a boil. Add 2 Tbs. broth from bok choy along with 2 Tbs. butter. Put bok choy in broth water and cook about 4 minutes or until tender. Remove and drain. To serve, place bok choy on plate, lay a piece of fish on top, and whisk sauce and spoon around fish. Sprinkle with toasted sesame seeds.

Footnote: To toast sesame seeds, place seeds in small dry skillet and turn heat to medium, stirring seeds until golden brown in color. Remove to a small bowl and let cool.

# *Coconut Shrimp with Chili Lime Sauce*

*This is great for an appetizer. I usually put it out on my buffet table along with the dipping sauce. Delicious! You might need more shrimp!*

16 extra large shrimp peeled, deveined and tail intact
2 Tbs. **Coconut Balsamic Vinegar**
1 cup flaked coconut
½ cup panko breadcrumbs
½ cup all purpose flour
1 large egg, beaten
1 Tbs. water
Vegetable oil for deep fat frying

**Chili Lime Dipping Sauce**
¼ cup fresh lime juice
1 cup Asian Sweet Chili Sauce (in supermarkets)
1 tsp. **Sesame Oil**
2 scallions minced plus some for decoration
¼ cup chopped fresh cilantro

In a large bowl add shrimp to coconut balsamic. In a shallow bowl add flaked coconut, breadcrumbs and flour and mix to combine. In another bowl add egg mixed with water. Dip shrimp in egg mixture then roll in breadcrumb mixture. In a deep heavy pot, heat oil to 375 degrees. Add shrimp a few at a time and do not overcrowd. Fry until golden brown, about 3 minutes. Drain on paper towels. Meanwhile in another bowl mix all ingredients for dipping sauce. Let sit at room temperature until ready to serve. Place shrimp on a large platter. Place dipping sauce in a small bowl alongside shrimp. Sprinkle minced scallions over shrimp to decorate.

# *Pecan Crusted Snapper w/ Pineapple Salsa*

*The tropical salsa is a perfect addition to this fish dish. It's a light and delicious entrée for summer. You can also replace pecans with pistachios or walnuts.*

Serves 4

4 (6 oz.) red snapper fillets
2 ripe mangos, pitted and diced
1 (20 oz.) can pineapple diced with juice
½ cup diced red pepper
¼ cup minced red onion
2 Tbs. fresh lime juice
3 Tbs. **Pineapple Balsamic Vinegar**
2 jalapeno peppers, seeds removed, minced
¼ cup chopped cilantro + sprigs for garnish
1 Tbs. chopped mint leaves
1 large egg
½ cup pecans, finely ground
½ cup plain breadcrumbs
1 T. all purpose four
2 Tbs. **Cilantro Roasted Onion Extra Virgin Olive Oil**
Salt and pepper to taste
Salt and pepper
1 box couscous

Put diced mango in a large bowl. Drain pineapple and reserve juice. Add pineapple to the bowl with the mango and add red pepper, red onion, lime juice, balsamic, jalapeno, chopped cilantro, and mint leaves. Add ¼ cup pineapple juice and mix gently. Refrigerate for at least 2 hours. Allow salsa mixture to come to room temperature before serving. Preheat oven to 350 degrees. Salt and pepper fish filets. In a small bowl, beat egg with 2 Tbs. water. Put nuts in grinder or processor and pulse until like fine crumbs. Place in bowl and add breadcrumbs and flour. Mix together and place on a large flat plate. Heat olive oil in skillet over medium heat. Dip fish in egg and coat with nut mixture on plate. Add fish to skillet and cook until golden brown on one side, about 4 minutes, turn and cook another 4 minutes. Place fish on a baking sheet and bake for 10 -15 minutes. Make couscous according to directions for servings needed. To plate, put couscous on individual plate, place a filet on top and spoon salsa with some liquid over fish. Top each with a sprig of cilantro.

**Cook's Note**
Salsa can be refrigerated and used on pork or grilled chicken. Snapper can be replaced with Tilapia, Striped Bass or Grouper. Fish times vary depending upon thickness of fish. You can substitute Mango Balsamic Vinegar for the Pineapple Balsamic Vinegar.

# *Pasta with Sun Dried Tomatoes and Olives*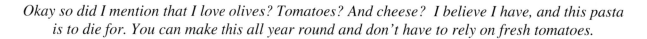

*Okay so did I mention that I love olives? Tomatoes? And cheese? I believe I have, and this pasta is to die for. You can make this all year round and don't have to rely on fresh tomatoes.*

**Serves 4**

3 Tbs. **Garlic Extra Virgin Olive Oil**
1 large clove garlic, minced
¾ cup finely chopped onion
6-8 sundried tomatoes packed in oil
1 lb. linguine pasta
1 cup low sodium chicken broth
½ cup Kalamata olives sliced
3 oz. goat cheese, crumbled
1/3 cup chopped basil
Cooked boneless marinated chicken (optional)

**Cook's Note**
Put 1 ½ cups of diced chicken breast with 3 Tbs. Aged Balsamic Vinegar in a bowl and let marinate for 10 minutes before adding to pasta. You can also add 1 jar of marinated artichokes hearts, drained and cut in half. Substitute the Slow Roasted Tomatoes (recipe on page 129), for the sundried tomatoes.

Add olive oil to a skillet over medium heat. Stir in garlic and onions and cook until onions are soft. Chop sun dried tomatoes and add to onions. Add broth and stir in olives and turn heat down to low. Boil water for pasta and cook according to directions until al dente. Drain well, reserving about ½ cup pasta water. In a small bowl add the ½ cup of pasta water and the goat cheese. Whisk until melted and smooth. Put pasta in a large bowl and add cheese sauce and broth mixture, and toss well. Mix in basil leaves and cooked marinated chicken and toss lightly. Add a little more olive oil if necessary. Serve hot.

# *Harissa Chicken Kabobs with Yogurt Sauce*

*This is a great grilling summer meal.  The addition of the yogurt sauce turns down the heat a bit.*

**Serves 6**

¾ cup **Harissa Extra Virgin Olive Oil**
¼ cup **Cinnamon Pear Balsamic Vinegar**
1 tsp. salt
2 garlic cloves, crushed
½ tsp. ground cumin
8 large chicken breasts
½ red onion cut into 1 ½" pieces
1 red pepper, cut into 1 ½" pieces
1 green pepper, cut into 1 ½ " pieces

**Yogurt Sauce**
2 (6 oz.) containers plain Greek style yogurt
1 clove garlic, minced
½ tsp. salt
Freshly ground black pepper
¼ tsp. cumin
2 Tbs. minced mint leaves
1 Tbs. lemon juice

Place olive oil, vinegar, salt, garlic and cumin in a bowl and whisk.  Cut chicken breasts into 1 ½" cubes. Place marinade in large bowl, add chicken and cover with plastic wrap or add marinate and chicken to a zip lock bag. Let marinate in refrigerator for 2 hours. Meanwhile if you are using wooden skewers then soak them in water for at least 30 minutes.  After 2 hours remove chicken from marinade, reserving marinade. Take a skewer and thread on a piece of chicken, an onion piece, a red pepper piece and a green pepper piece and continue like that until skewer is almost at full to end. Fill at least 6 kabobs. Puree reserved marinade in blender.  Place in a bowl and set aside. To make yogurt sauce, mix all sauce ingredients in a bowl and keep in refrigerator until use.  Add more salt and pepper if needed. Place kabobs on an oiled hot grill and cook about 8 minutes on one side.  Brush a little reserved marinade onto kabobs, turn and cook another 5-8 minutes. Remove to a platter. Discard leftover marinade. Let rest 5 minutes before serving.  Pass the yogurt sauce in a bowl or spoon some over the kabobs.  Serve over Cucumber Couscous. (Recipe on page 49 ).

# *Lemon Roasted Chicken with Vegetables*

*To me nothing is better than a whole roasted chicken. It is comfort food that I never tire of. I have added some roasted vegetables for a complete all in one meal. The chicken has a nice lemony taste and the balsamic is a nice touch to this favorite.*

**Serves 4**

1 3-4 lb. whole roasting chicken
8 sprigs of fresh thyme
3-4 sage leaves
2 3" sprigs of rosemary
1 lemon, cut in half
1 onion, cut in half
2 Tbs. **Eureka Lemon Extra Virgin Olive Oil**
5 large cloves garlic, peeled and cut in half
1 generous cup, cut and peeled baby carrots
4 small-medium size new potatoes, quartered
1 ½ cup peeled and cut into 2" pieces parsnips
½ tsp. coarse **Rosemary Sea Salt**
freshly ground pepper
1 Tbs. **18 Year Aged Balsamic Vinegar**

**Cook's Note:**
You can substitute plain sea salt for the Rosemary sea salt.

Preheat oven to 400 degrees. Set rack in middle of oven. Remove innards from chicken and cut off any large lumps of fat. Wash inside and out and pat dry. Loosen skin under breast. Stuff this with 4 sprigs of thyme, sage leaves and 1 sprig of rosemary. Stuff cavity with both lemon halves and one half of onion. Prick skin slightly. Lightly grease a roasting pan with some lemon olive oil. Place rest of herbs in center and lay chicken on top. In a bowl add garlic, carrots, potatoes, parsnips and other half of onion quartered along with 1 Tbs. lemon oil and some black pepper. Mix to coat and add these around chicken in pan. Take 1 Tbs. lemon oil and rub over chicken. Sprinkle the rosemary salt over the chicken and vegetables. Roast for 30 minutes. Baste after 15 minutes with collected juices. Lower heat to 375 degrees and cook for another one hour, basting frequently. Check temperature of bird by inserting meat thermometer into thickest part of thigh. Temperature should read 165 degrees. Sprinkle balsamic over top of bird and cook another 5 minutes. Remove chicken and let rest 10 minutes before carving. Remove vegetables to a platter. Cover with foil to keep warm. Discard herb sprigs from pan and remove fat from sauce. Add more salt and pepper if needed. Carve chicken into 8 pieces or 4 quarters. Place on platter with vegetables and serve the gravy alongside in a gravy boat.

# *Chicken with Figs*

*Adapted from Daisy Martinez' recipe, this shortcut version includes the addition of fig balsamic which brings out a wonderful richness in this dish. If you want to cut down on the fat, you can take the skin off the chicken.*

**Serves 4**

1 (4 lb.) chicken cut up, washed and dried
6 slices lean bacon cut into 1" pieces
3 Tbs. **Hojiblanca Extra Virgin Olive Oil**
½ onion, cut into 1" pieces
2 stalk celery, cut into 1" pieces
2 carrots, cut into 1" pieces
4 cloves garlic chopped
2 Tbs. flour
1 Tbs. tomato paste
1 (25 oz.) box chicken stock
1 (25 oz.) box beef stock
¼ cup **Fig Balsamic Vinegar**
3 sprigs parsley plus more for garnishing
3 thyme sprigs
1 bay leaf
1 4 lb. chicken cut up, washed and dried
12 oz. or 2 cups dried mission figs
¼ cup Port or Sherry wine

**Cook's Note**
If you can't find dried mission figs, dried Calimyrna figs or fresh figs will work fine. Any medium intensity Spanish Olive Oil can be used in place of Hojiblanca. To remove oil, from stew, place a paper towel gently over top of stew and let it absorb fat. Repeat until desired.

Cook bacon in large pot until brown but not so crispy. Remove with slotted spoon and place on paper towels to drain. Remove all but 1 Tbs. of bacon fat from pot and add 1 Tbs. olive oil along with onions, celery and carrots. Cook until slightly brown, about 10 minutes. Add garlic and cook 2 minutes then add flour and stir. Cook for 1 minute. Add tomato paste and stir constantly for 1 minute. Remove pan from heat and stir in the chicken and beef stock. Bring to boil then reduce heat and add vinegar, parsley and thyme and bay leaf. Let simmer uncovered for 45 minutes. Meanwhile, cut stems off figs and place in bowl and cover with boiling water. Let sit on counter until figs have softened, about 20 minutes. Discard liquid and cut figs in half lengthwise. Heat 2 Tbs. oil in a skillet or deep sauté pan. Salt and pepper chicken pieces and add to skillet, but do not crowd. Lightly brown on one side for 8-10 minutes over medium heat turn over and lightly brown on other side. Remove pieces and brown second batch in same way. Place in bowl and set aside. Remove cooked sauce from stovetop and put through a strainer over a bowl, pushing down on solids. Set sauce aside. Scrape up brown bits in pan that chicken was browned in. Add Port and cook for 1 minute, scraping solids. Add to the pan, 4 -5 cups of reserved sauce along with figs, chicken pieces and reserved bacon. Bring to a boil, turn heat down to low to medium heat and cover with lid. Cook for about 1 ½ hours. Remove oil from top of stew. Salt and pepper if needed. Serve on individual plates or on a large platter. Sprinkle with chopped parsley.

# *Grilled Chipotle Chicken and Peaches*

*The smoky spicy flavored chicken matches beautifully with the sweet fruitiness of the peaches. Yum!*

*Serves 4*

1 lb. boneless chicken breasts (4 pieces)
2 chipotles in adobo sauce
¼ cup **Chipotle Extra Virgin Olive Oil**
2 Tbs. fresh lemon juice
1 tsp. minced garlic
3 Tbs. honey
2 Tbs. **18 Year Aged Balsamic Vinegar**
1 Tbs. dried oregano
4 almost ripe peaches, pitted and halved

Vinaigrette:
3 Tbs. **Peach White Balsamic Vinegar**
1 Tbs. minced shallots
1 tsp. Dijon mustard
½ cup fruity **Extra Virgin Olive Oil (Hojiblanca)**
1 (10 oz.) package baby arugula
3 oz. blue cheese, crumbled

**Cook's Note**
Do not use canned peaches. Use only fresh peaches in season.

Wash and dry chicken breasts. If over 1 inch thick then pound them to 1 inch. Set aside. To make marinade, mince chipotles and place in food processor with olive oil, lemon juice, garlic, honey, vinegar, and oregano. Puree and taste. Add some salt if needed. Put the chicken in a zip lock bag or glass dish, add marinade and refrigerate for one hour. Remove chicken and reserve the marinade. Dry chicken and set grill on medium high or use a skillet. Oil grill grates and cook chicken 3-4 minutes on one side. Turn chicken clockwise to get crisscross grill patterns. Continue cooking on that side for 4-5 more minutes. Turn chicken over and repeat the process. Remove from grill and let rest for about 10 minutes. Re oil the grill grates, brush cut side of peaches with some Hojiblanca olive oil and grill about 5-7 minutes, check to make sure they are not burning. Remove and set aside to cool.

To make Vinaigrette, put vinegar, shallots and mustard in bowl. Whisk in olive oil in a steady stream to thicken and emulsify. Add salt and pepper to taste.
Put arugula in a large salad bowl and add vinaigrette. Toss well. Divide salad into 4 plates. Slice peaches and place on top of arugula. Slice chicken and lay on top of peaches. Sprinkle with blue cheese.

# *Lavender Balsamic Chicken*

*This chicken can be cooked in the oven or grilled on the barbecue.  For a spring or summer menu pair this with potato salad.*

Serves 4

4 boneless chicken breasts (about 5-6 oz. each)
¼ cup **Lavender Balsamic Vinegar**
2 Tbs. **Herbs de Provence Extra Virgin Olive Oil**
1 tsp. minced fresh Rosemary
3 cloves garlic, crushed
1 tsp. lemon juice
½ cup low salt chicken broth
2 Tbs. honey
1 tsp.Dijon mustard
1 tsp. salt
1/8 tsp. freshly grinded black pepp
1/8 tsp. cayenne pepper
1 tsp. dried lavender leaves (optional)

Place chicken breasts in zip lock bag.  In a bowl combine rest of ingredients, whisking until mixed.  Add to chicken in zip lock and refrigerate for about 2 hours, turning bag every few hours.  Remove chicken from bag, discard marinade. Place chicken on a baking sheet lined with aluminum foil. Bake at 350 degrees for about 40 minutes or until a thermometer when inserted into thickest part of chicken reads 165 degrees.  Remove from oven and let rest 5 minutes before serving. Slice chicken into ½" slices to serve.

**Cook's Note**
Serve this with Potato Salad Vinaigrette or Sweet Potato Oven Fries. The recipes are in the book.  Serve on a salad and you have a nice seasonal dinner.  To grill chicken, oil grates and lay chicken on grill about 12-15 minutes each side.  You can also use this recipe on pork or lamb. Check the cooking temperatures in back of book.

#  Desserts

#  Desserts

# Black Cherry and Almond Biscotti

*These buttery cherry flavored cookies are fairly easy to make. The recipe makes plenty and it's a good thing because these will disappear quickly.*

**Makes about 50**

2 cups sugar
1 cup (2 sticks) unsalted butter, room temperature
4 large eggs
4 ½ cups flour
4 tsp. baking powder
1 tsp. salt
¼ cup brandy
3 Tbs. **Black Cherry Balsamic Vinegar**
Plus extra for dipping
1 ½ tsp. vanilla extract
1 cup whole almonds, toasted
1 cup dried cranberries or dried cherries

Preheat oven to 350 degrees. Line 2 heavy large baking sheets with foil. Beat sugar and butter in electric mixer until light and fluffy. Add eggs one at a time, beating well after each addition. Mix flour, baking powder, and salt in medium bowl. Combine brandy, vinegar and vanilla extract in a glass measuring cup. Add dry ingredients and brandy mixture alternately to sugar mixture, beginning and ending with dry ingredients. Stir in almonds and cranberries. Drop dough by spoonfuls onto the prepared baking sheets, forming two, 2" wide and 13" long strips on each baking sheet. Moisten fingertips and smooth dough into logs. Bake until golden and firm to touch about 40 minutes. Transfer sheets to racks to cool completely. Reduce oven to 300 degrees. Transfer cooled logs to work surface. Using a serrated knife, cut logs into diagonal ¾ " slices. Arrange on baking sheets. Bake cookies until dry, and slightly browned, turning every 10 minutes, about 40 minutes total. Transfer to racks to cool. To serve put some extra balsamic in a bowl and have guests dip biscotti ends.

103

# *Rustic Apple Butter Tart*

*This tart is rustic in appearance but the flavors are very sophisticated. The use of premade puff pastry makes this an easy recipe to prepare. Try the ice cream as a topping! Oh Boy!*

**Makes 1 tart or 4 individual tarts**

4-5 granny smith apples, peeled and cored
1 Tbs. butter
3 Tbs. sugar
½ tsp. ground cinnamon
1 good quality frozen puff pastry sheet, defrosted
Tbs. **Maple Balsamic Vinegar**
¼ cup **Braswells's Apple Butter**

1 pint good quality vanilla ice cream
1 tsp. Calvados, Applejack or Dark Rum

Preheat oven to 400 degrees. Cut apples in half and into 5 wedges from each half. Place butter in skillet and add 2 Tbs. sugar along with cinnamon. Saute until golden brown, about 8-10 minutes. Remove from heat. Flour a wooden board and roll out puff pastry to a 12" round. (Use a large dinner plate as your template and knife around edge. Remove plate). Transfer pastry round to a baking sheet. In a small bowl mix the vinegar with apple butter. Spread apple butter mixture into center of pastry leaving 2-3" border from edge of dough. Place apple mixture on top and fold excess dough over apples, leaving center apples exposed. Pinch dough to seal. Sprinkle over top and edges with 1 Tbs. sugar. Bake for 30-40 minutes. Cool. Serve with ice cream if desired.

**Cook's Note**
You can make 4 individual tarts by rolling out puff pastry into a 12 inch square and dividing that into 4 equal squares, leaving a ¾ inch border. Proceed same way as recipe. If using ice cream, put in bowl. Soften ice cream slightly by mixing with spoon. Mix in the Calvados, put back in container and refreeze until use.

# *Blood Orange Olive Oil Cake*

*This is an easy and delicious cake which shouts orange. It goes great with a cup of coffee or tea. Make this recipe for a breakfast, lunch or dinner dessert.*

**Makes 1 cake**

1 Tbs. butter
4 large eggs
1 cup granulated sugar
3 cups flour + some for dusting
1 Tbs. baking powder
Grated zest of one orange
¾ cup **Blood Orange Extra Virgin Olive Oil**
1/3 cup milk
1/3 cup fresh orange juice
1 tsp. vanilla extract

**Glaze:**
¼ cup fresh orange juice
¼ cup granulated sugar
2 Tbs. Gran Marnier liquor
Confectionary sugar for dusting

Preheat oven to 325 degrees. Butter an 11 cup bundt pan and dust with flour. Set aside. Beat eggs and sugar in bowl of electric mixer on high until pale yellow and fluffy, about 5-8 minutes. Add remaining 3 cups of flour, baking powder, orange zest, oil, milk, orange juice and vanilla and stir until well combined. Spoon batter into prepared bundt pan and smooth on top. Bake about 40 minutes until golden (top will split slightly), and cake tester comes out clean when inserted into center of cake. Transfer pan to rack and let cool. In a small saucepan combine orange juice and sugar and simmer stirring until sugar is dissolved. Add Gran Marnier and let simmer until slightly syrupy. Remove cake from pan and place on rack with wax paper underneath to catch drippings when glazing. Poke holes in top of cake with cake tester and slowly brush or pour glaze over top and sides of cake. Let cool completely and dust with confectioner's sugar. Serve.

**Cook's Note**
This cake stays fresh if made the day before and wrapped in aluminum foil. Can also be frozen and defrosted when ready to use.

# Coconut Balsamic Ambrosia

*This tropical fruit dessert is creamy and has wonderful coconut undertones. Treat yourself and others to this refreshing dessert. It's lower in calories than other ambrosias. A perfect ending to a lovely spring or summer meal.*

**Serves 6-8**

1 can (20 oz.) pineapple chunks, drained
1 can (15 oz.) mandarin oranges, drained
1 can (15 oz.) tropical fruit mix, drained
2 bananas, sliced
1 cup seedless red grapes
2 Tbs. **Coconut Balsamic Vinegar**
12 oz. fat free plain Greek style yogurt
½ cup flaked coconut plus ½ cup for toasting
1 ½ cup miniature marshmallows

Place pineapple, oranges, tropical fruit mix, bananas, and grapes in a large bowl. Fold in yogurt, ½ cup of coconut flakes and all of marshmallows. Cover with plastic wrap and refrigerate for at least I hour. Serve in individual bowls, cups or glasses and add a sprinkling of toasted coconut on top.

**To toast coconut:** Preheat oven to 325 degrees. Spread coconut flakes on ungreased baking sheet. Check often, every few minutes to insure that coconut is not burning. Watch closely and stir often. Coconut should be light brown in color. Remove from oven and let cool. It can be stored in a plastic container or jar at room temperature.

**Cook's Note**
The thickness of the Greek style yogurt is the secret to keeping this ambrosia from becoming watery. This ambrosia keeps well in your refrigerator.

# *Poached Pears with Balsamic and Mascarpone Whipped Cream*

*It is important that your pears are not over ripe. Look for ones that are not soft yet not hard. The mascarpone cream can be used for many different desserts. Yum!*

**Serves 4**

1 ¼ cups granulated sugar
2 cups apple juice
2 cups water
4 pears, not too ripe
1 tsp. vanilla extract
1 Tbs. finely grated fresh ginger
½ tsp. ground cinnamon
3 Tbs. **Cinnamon Pear Balsamic Vinegar**
Grated zest of 1 lemon
8 oz. heavy cream, cold
2 oz. Mascarpone cheese (room Temperature)
1 Tbs. confectioner's sugar

Put sugar and apple juice along with water in heavy saucepan over medium heat. Stir constantly to dissolve sugar. Peel each pear, core and cut in half from top to bottom or lengthwise. Bring syrup to boil and add pears. Add vanilla, ginger, cinnamon, vinegar and lemon zest. Turn down heat and simmer uncovered over low heat for 40-50 minutes or until pears are tender. Lift out with slotted spoon. Put pears on platter and cover loosely with plastic wrap and refrigerate. Let poaching liquid cool in pot. When cooled, transfer pears from platter to a bowl and add poaching liquid. Put back in refrigerator for several hours or overnight. Before serving whip heavy cream in a bowl until soft peaks. Add room temperature cheese and confectioner's sugar. Continue whipping until stiff peaks. To serve, place 2 pear halves on plate and pour some poaching liquid over top. Top with dollop of whipped cream mixture and a tiny sprinkling of cinnamon.

# *Tangy Cheesecake with Berry Coulis*

*This is a creamy cheesecake with a wonderful sweet berry topping. The cheesecake can be made in the morning or the day before serving.*

20 graham crackers
½ tsp. cinnamon
9 Tbs. unsalted butter, melted
4 ounces mascarpone cheese, room temperature
5 ounces creamy goat cheese, room temperature
2 cups crème fraiche, room temperature
3 eggs, room temperature
1 cup granulated sugar
1 Tbs. finely grated zest of lemon
2 Tbs. fresh lemon juice
½ tsp. vanilla extract

**Berry Coulis**
3 ½ cups strawberries, hulled and halved
1 Tbs. fresh lemon juice
3 Tbs. superfine sugar
¼ cup **Strawberry Zinfandel Balsamic Glaze**
1 pint raspberries

**Cook's Note**
To make crème fraiche:  In a bowl add I cup sour cream and add to that 1 cup heavy cream.  Whisk to combine and thicken slightly.  Place into a glass jar and cover with plastic wrap.  Leave on kitchen counter overnight.  Cream will get thicker.  Place in refrigerator and chill at least 12 hours.

Heat oven to 325 degrees.  Wrap the outside of a 10 inch springform pan with aluminum foil.  In a food processor add graham crackers, cinnamon and butter and pulse until crackers are finely ground and mixture hold together.  Press into the bottom of the springform pan.  Chill until ready to use.  Clean processor and add mascarpone, goat cheese, crème fraiche, eggs, sugar, lemon zest, lemon juice and vanilla.  Mix until smooth, scraping down sides.  Pour into prepared springform pan and place pan into a large roasting pan and surround springform with hot water, reaching about 1 ½ inches up the sides of the pan.  Bake for 45 minutes or until sides look firm and center has a slight jiggle.  Cake tester should come out clean when inserted into the center.  Remove from oven and let cool in pan while still in water bath.  Remove from roasting pan and let cake cool in springform pan at room temperature for another 15 minutes.  Chill cake in springform pan in refrigerator for about 8 hours.  To make coulis, add to a food processor 1 ½ cups of strawberries, lemon juice and sugar.  Pulse until smooth.  Strain the berry mixture into a bowl and add the balsamic glaze.  Mix in the 2 ½ cups of fresh strawberries and raspberries.  Place in refrigerator until use.  To serve unmold cheesecake and slice into servings placing berry mixture on top of each slice.

# *Pumpkin Spice Muffins w/ Streusel Tops*

*The flavors of the combined spices, the moist texture and the added topping make these muffins so delicious that you might have to hide them and keep them just for yourself. A good cup of tea or coffee and you will truly relax.*

**Makes 1 dozen**

2 cups all purpose flour
¼ tsp. baking powder
1 tsp. baking soda
1 tsp. ground cinnamon
¼ tsp. ground ginger
¼ tsp. ground cloves
¼ tsp. ground nutmeg
½ tsp. salt
¾ cup light brown sugar
¼ cup white granulated sugar
¼ cup + 2 Tbs. **Organic Butter Extra Virgin Olive Oil**
2 large eggs
½ cup low fat milk (1 % or 2%)
2 Tbs. **Pumpkin Spice Balsamic Vinegar**
1 cup solid packed pumpkin puree
1 tsp. vanilla extract
½ cup semisweet chocolate chips

**Streusel Topping**
½ cup all purpose flour
1/3 cup light brown sugar
¼ cup chopped walnuts
½ tsp. ground cinnamon
3 Tbs. unsalted butter, room temperature

Preheat oven to 375 degrees. Line a 12 cup muffin tin with cupcake paper liner cups. In a large bowl mix the dry ingredients. In another bowl whisk together the olive oil, eggs, milk, vinegar, pumpkin puree and vanilla. Add wet ingredients to dry mixture and stir until well combined. Fold in chocolate chips. Spoon batter into cups almost filling to top. In another bowl add all dry streusel ingredients. Add butter and incorporate with fingers until crumbly. Sprinkle topping over the batter in cups. Bake 20 minutes or until a toothpick or cake tester when inserted into the center of muffin comes out clean. Remove from oven and let cool before serving.

**Footnote**
You can bake this mixture in a loaf pan instead of the muffin tins. Cooking time may be extended by 10 minutes. Keep checking with cake tester.

110

# *White Chocolate Mousse And Balsamic Berry Parfait*

*The combination of the sweet chocolate mousse combined with the tartness of the glazed berries make this dessert not only pretty but memorable.*

**Makes 6**

¾ tsp. unflavored gelatin
3 Tbs. water
8 oz. good quality white chocolate chips
1 ½ cups heavy cream, chilled
1 pint strawberries, hulled and halved
¾ cup blackberries
1 ½ cups raspberries
1/3 cup **Strawberry Zinfandel Balsamic Glaze**
Sifted powdered sugar for decoration

Put water in bowl and sprinkle top with gelatin. Let stand for 5 minutes until softened. Set aside. Place chocolate in a heatproof bowl and set aside. Place ½ cup of heavy cream into a small saucepan and bring to a boil. Remove from heat and add the softened gelatin, and stir until combined. Immediately pour over chocolate and let sit 1 minute. Stir until smooth. Refrigerate chocolate mixture until cold and thick, about 30-40 minutes. In a bowl add washed and drained berries and 1/3 cup of balsamic glaze. Put in refrigerator until use. In another bowl, whisk the chilled 1 cup of heavy cream until stiff peaks. Fold into the chocolate mixture. Place in refrigerator until serving.

To serve, place a small paper doilie on a dessert plate and place a wine glass on top. Put about 2 Tbs. of berry mixture into bottom of glass and add 1/6 of chocolate mousse on top. Top with 1/6 of rest of berries. Repeat for 5 more wine glasses. Sprinkle tops with powdered sugar and serve.

**Cook's Note**
If chocolate is not smooth enough then place the chocolate filled bowl in a bath of hot water and continue stirring until smooth.

# *Chocolate Mocha Mousse*

*This is a rich chocolaty coffee flavored mousse. The addition of cognac makes it entirely decadent. You will need a few mixing bowls for this.*

**Serves 6**

3 large eggs, separated
¾ cup + 1 Tbs. superfine sugar
2 Tbs. cognac or brandy
1 tsp. vanilla extract
5 ounces good quality bittersweet chocolate
4 Tbs. unsalted butter, room temperature
1 Tbs. **Espresso Balsamic Vinegar**
2 Tbs. strong coffee
½ cup heavy cream

Extra whipped cream for decoration
Extra chocolate for decoration

In an electric mixer beat egg yolks with ¾ cup sugar. Add cognac and vanilla and continue beating until mixture is thick and pale yellow. Place mixture on stove on top of double boiler over barely simmering water, and continue to heat while beating until mixture is foamy, about 5 minutes. Remove pot from simmering water and let it come to room temperature. In another pot melt chocolate. (You can also do this in microwave. See footnote below). Remove and stir in butter. Add chocolate mixture to egg mixture and stir with a wooden spoon until smooth and creamy. Stir in balsamic and coffee. Set aside. In a large bowl whip egg whites until foamy. Sprinkle additional Tbs. of sugar over whites and continue beating until stiff peaks. Fold ¼ of egg whites into chocolate mixture to incorporate. Then fold rest of mixture gently but thoroughly making sure no white streaks show. Set aside. In another bowl, whip the cream. Fold into chocolate mixture. You can serve this in individual bowls or in one big bowl. Refrigerate for at least 4 hours before serving. Before serving whip some cream and place a small dollop on top of mousse and shave a little chocolate over top.

**Cook's Note**
The addition of the whipped cream and shaved chocolate as a decoration will add richness to an already rich dessert.

**Footnote:** To melt chocolate in microwave, place broken pieces of chocolate in a heatproof glass measuring cup and place in microwave on high for 30 seconds. Remove and stir. Replace in microwave for another 30 seconds and continue this pattern until chocolate is melted.

113

# *Peach Tart in Cinnamon Almond Crust*

*This is a tasty tart made with fresh peaches which is sure to please. Serve with a scoop of vanilla ice cream on top and try to eat just one slice!*

**Makes 1 (9-inch) Tart**

¼ cup slivered almonds
½ cup powdered sugar
Pinch of salt
1 ¼ cups all purpose flour, chilled
1 ½ teaspoons ground cinnamon
1 large egg yolk
5-6 ripe peaches
4 Tblsp. granulated sugar
½ cup (1 stick) unsalted butter, chilled, cut into ½" pieces plus 3 Tblsp. unsalted butter
½ cup **Braswell's Apricot Peach Preserves**
1 Tblsp. **Peach White Balsamic Vinegar**
Vanilla ice cream (optional)

Finely grind almonds in a food processor. Add powdered sugar, salt, flour, and cinnamon and pulse to combine. Add egg yolk and butter and pulse until the dough forms a ball. Add a teaspoon of ice water at a time if needed. Flatten dough into a disk and wrap in plastic wrap. Refrigerate for at least 1 hour. Remove dough and using fingers press dough into bottom and sides of a greased 9" tart pan with a removable bottom. Freeze tart for 10–15 minutes. Preheat oven to 400 degrees. Cut peaches into ¼" slices and arrange in concentric circles to fit snugly into the tart. Sprinkle with sugar and dot with the 3 Tbs. of butter. Bake for 40 -50 minutes until crust is nicely browned and sugar is caramelized. If crust is getting too brown, then place aluminum foil over tart until cooked. Heat preserves in a small saucepan and add balsamic. Stir until melted. Remove tart from oven, brush with preserve mixture and place tart in pan on top of rack to cool. Remove rim and place on cake plate. Slice and serve with a scoop of ice cream.

# Crepes with Balsamic Berries

*These crepes are so light and lacy that you can stuff them with just about anything. You can change the balsamic; just make sure you use the white balsamic. You can also replace the balsamic with Grand Marnier. Do invest in a crepe pan if you don't have one.*

**Makes 8 crepes**

3 large eggs
1 cup whole milk
1 tsp. vanilla extract
3 Tbs. unsalted butter melted
1 Tbs. **Apricot Balsamic Vinegar**
1 cup cornstarch
1/8 tsp. salt
3 Tbs. superfine sugar
1 Tbs. clarified butter (or cooking spray)
½ pint strawberries, hulled and halved or quartered
½ pint blueberries
½ pint raspberries
¼ cup **Blueberry Balsamic Vinegar**
Vanilla ice cream
**Blueberry Balsamic Glaze** (in back of book)

Place eggs, milk, vanilla extract, melted butter, vinegar, cornstarch, salt and 1 Tbs. of the sugar in a blender or food processor and mix until smooth, about 10 to 15 seconds. Place crepe pan or nonstick crepe pan, on stovetop over high heat. (Pan must be very hot). Brush a small amount of clarified butter in the pan or use cooking spray. Pour ¼ cup or less of batter in pan and quickly tilt pan in all directions to coat entire bottom of pan. Cook until you see bubbles popping under batter and sides of crepe begin to lightly brown. Flip over with a spatula and cook another 30-45 seconds. Have a plate ready with wax paper cut in large squares. Place crepes between sheets of wax paper and let cool. Place berries in a large bowl and add 2 Tbs. sugar and balsamic vinegar. Mix gently and place in refrigerator for 1 hour. When ready to serve, place 1 scoop of vanilla ice cream into center of the crepe. Roll into a log shape and place berries on and around it. Drizzle or dot the blueberry glaze around the plate. Serve cold.

**Cook's note:**
You can stuff the crepes with lemon curd whipped cream, mascarpone whipped cream, white chocolate mousse, or butter pecan ice cream In place of the vanilla ice cream. You can also double the crepe recipe for more servings.

**Footnote**
To clarify butter put ¼ cup unsalted butter in a small saucepan and melt butter over medium heat. The milk solids will rise to the top. When thy do scoop them out with a small strainer leaving just the clear butter. Let cool before using.

115

# *Banana Walnut Bread*

*If you like the taste of bananas you'll love this loaf. It is moist and can be served as dessert or a breakfast treat.*

**Makes 1 loaf**

½ cup light brown sugar
½ cup granulated sugar
¼ cup walnut oil
2 large eggs, beaten
½ cup sour cream
4 ripe bananas (2 cups mashed)
1 tsp. vanilla extract
2 cups flour
1 tsp. baking soda
½ tsp. baking powder
½ tsp. salt
½ tsp. cinnamon
½ cup chopped toasted walnuts

Preheat oven to 350 degrees. Grease and flour a 9 x 5 inch glass loaf pan. Beat sugars and oil together in bowl of an electric mixer until well blended. Add eggs, sour cream, bananas and vanilla. Blend well. In another bowl sift flour, baking soda, baking powder, salt and cinnamon and stir until mixed. Add dry ingredients to wet ones in bowl and mix until incorporated. Fold in nuts. Pour batter into prepared loaf pan and bake for 80-90 minutes or until a cake tester when inserted into center comes out clean. Remove from oven and place pan on rack for 10 minutes. Remove bread from pan and continue to cool on rack.

**Cook's Note**
If using a tin loaf pan, reduce oven cooking time by 20 to 30 minutes. To toast walnuts place in ungreased non stick skillet on medium heat, while occasionally shaking pan, and cook until fragrant and light brown. Do not burn. Remove and let cool.

# *Almond Oil Lemon Cake*

*With the great roasted almond flavor and lemony glaze, this light cake will sure to please. It's simple to make and bakes rather quickly.*

**Makes 1 cake**

1½ cups flour
2 tsp. baking powder
½ tsp. salt
1 cup sugar
3 large eggs
Zest of one orange
Zest of 2 lemons
¼ cup milk
½ tsp. vanilla extract
½ cup + 2 Tbs. **Roasted Almond Oil**
2 Tbs. **Eureka Lemon Extra Virgin Olive Oil**
Confectioner's sugar for dusting

**Glaze**
¼ cup lemon juice
¼ cup granulated sugar
2 Tbs. Lemoncello liquor

Preheat oven to 350 degrees. Lightly oil a bundt pan and set aside. Mix flour, baking powder and salt in bowl. With electric mixer, beat sugar with eggs and zests, beating several minutes until pale and fluffy. Beat in milk and extract. Slowly add oils on high speed. Add flour mixture and mix well. Pour batter in prepared pan and bake about 35 minutes or when cake tester is inserted and comes out clean. Let cool in pan on rack. Meanwhile put lemon juice and sugar in saucepan on stovetop and stir until sugar is dissolved. Let cool and add Lemoncello. Poke holes into cake with cake tester and brush with glaze. Let sit for 15 minutes or more until cooled. Dust with powdered sugar.

# *Dark Chocolate Balsamic Tiramisu*

*This is an Italian favorite with a twist. The flavors are just mouth watering. Serve this dish to a small crowd. It will definitely please.*

Serves 8-10

5 yolks of large eggs
½ cup granulated sugar
1/3 cup dry Marsala
1 cup heavy cream
8 oz. Mascarpone cheese, room temperature
¾ cup strong brewed espresso with 1 Tbsp. sugar, cooled
3 Tbs. **Dark Chocolate Balsamic Vinegar**
2 Tbs. Tia Maria or Kahlua
½ tsp. vanilla extract
4 oz. bittersweet chocolate, chopped fine
24 lady fingers
Unsweetened cocoa powder for dusting

Whisk egg yolks and sugar in a bowl to blend. In a heavy saucepan over simmering water add egg mixture and Marsala. Whisk until tripled in volume, about 5-8 minutes. Remove from heat. In a bowl of a mixer, beat cream and mascarpone until stiff peaks form. Fold Marsala custard into whipped cream mixture until well incorporated. In another bowl put espresso, balsamic, Kahlua and vanilla extract. Stir. To assemble cake, place a layer of ladyfingers in a 9 x 13" glass baking pan. (You will use 12 ladyfingers halved). Brush with the espresso liquid until moist but not saturated. Spread ½ of the whipped cream mixture on top and sprinkle with ½ of the chocolate. Arrange another layer of brushed lady fingers on top and spread remaining whipped cream mixture. Refrigerate for at least 2 hours. Before serving, dust with cocoa powder and sprinkle with the rest of the chocolate.

119

Blueberry Balsamic Crumb Cake

# *Blueberry Balsamic Crumb Cake*

*One of my favorite berries is blueberries. This crumb cake is moist and quite easy to make. You can substitute the pine nuts with walnuts or pecans for a slightly different flavor.*

**Makes 1 cake**

1 ½ cup fresh blueberries
¼ cup **Blueberry Balsamic Vinegar**
6 Tbs. unsalted butter, room temperature
¾ cup granulated sugar
2 large eggs, room temperature
1 tsp. vanilla extract
1 tsp. grated lemon zest
6 oz. container Greek style plain yogurt
1 ¼ cups all purpose flour
1 tsp. baking powder
½ tsp. baking soda
½ tsp. salt

**Streusel Topping**:
½ cup flour
1/3 cup light brown sugar
¼ cup chopped pine nuts
1 tsp. cinnamon
3 Tbs. unsalted butter, softened
Confectioner's sugar for dusting

Preheat oven to 350 degrees. Butter and flour a 9" spring form pan and set aside. Place blueberries with vinegar in bowl and let sit for 20 minutes, stirring occasionally. Cream butter and sugar in bowl of mixer fitted with paddle attachment and beat on high for about 4 minutes until creamy and fluffy. Reduce speed to low add eggs one at a time mixing about 30 seconds each. Add vanilla and lemon zest and mix. Add yogurt and mix gently to incorporate. In a separate bowl, sift together the dry ingredients. Add flour mixture to batter until just combined. Drain blueberries, keeping vinegar for some other purpose. Fold blueberries into batter with a spatula making sure batter is completely mixed. Spoon batter into the prepared pan and spread evenly. Set aside. To make streusel, place flour, sugar, pine nuts and cinnamon in a bowl. Cut butter into 6 pieces, add to bowl and work with fingers to a crumbly texture. Sprinkle topping over batter. Bake for 40 minutes or until a cake tester when inserted comes out clean. Cool completely in pan and remove from spring form. Place on cake platter and dust with sifted confectioner's sugar.

# Raspberry Merlot Balsamic Sorbet

*This is a satisfying and refreshing raspberry sorbet. It's the perfect dessert for a special dinner or anytime you want to impress your friends.*

**Makes 1 quart**

1 cup granulated sugar
1 ½ cups water
2 cups (fresh raspberries)
1 (12 oz. bag) frozen raspberries, defrosted
1 tsp. lemon juice
¼ cup **Raspberry Merlot Balsamic Glaze**
Mint leaves for decoration.

Put sugar and water in a saucepan on high heat and stir until all sugar is dissolved. Remove from heat. When cooled, place in refrigerator for another hour. Put fresh and defrosted raspberries and lemon juice in food processor and puree. Place strainer over bowl and strain to remove seeds. Add cooled sugar water along with balsamic glaze. Mix thoroughly. Put in ice cream maker and follow their instructions. Place in plastic container with lid until use. To serve, place in separate bowls or wine glasses and decorate with a sprig of mint.

**Cook's Note**
If you do not have an ice cream maker you can spread the sorbet in a glass pan or shallow glass baking dish and place in freezer. Check in about 45 minutes and scrape the sorbet with a fork. Replace in freezer checking every half hour, scraping until desired consistency. Place in a plastic container with lid and keep in freezer until use.

# *Sauces, Stocks, Etc.*

# *Basil Oil Pesto*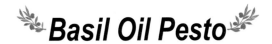

*This diversified pesto can be used on pasta, grilled meats, sandwiches, pizza or mozzarella and tomatoes.*

**Makes 2 cups**

4 cups basil leaves
½ cup grated Parmesan Reggiano cheese
½ cup grated Pecorino Romano cheese
2 cloves garlic, peeled
½ cup pine nuts, toasted
½ tsp. salt
½ cup **Basil Organic Extra Virgin Olive Oil**
3 Tbs. warm water

Wash basil leaves and dry between paper towels. Put cheeses in food processor and blend until finely ground. Set aside in a bowl. In same processor put basil leaves, garlic cloves, nuts, salt, olive oil, and water. Pulse until all ingredients are almost pureed. Remove from processor to a large bowl and stir in cheeses. If mixture is too thick then add more warm water. Store the pesto in a covered jar in refrigerator until use. It should stay fresh for about 2 weeks.

# *Tuscan Herb and Parmesan Croutons*

*These lovely little bites of cheesy croutons are great in any salad but especially good in the Caesar salad.*

1 loaf unseeded Italian bread, cut into ¾" cubes
¼ cup **Tuscan Herb Extra Virgin Olive Oil**
¼ cup **Garlic Extra Virgin Olive Oil**
½ tsp. salt
½ tsp. freshly ground pepper
¼ cup finely grated Parmesan cheese

Preheat oven to 350 degrees. Place cubes of bread in a large bowl. Add olive oils, salt and pepper and toss with hands to make sure all cubes are covered well. Spread cubes in a single layer onto 1 or 2 baking pans. Bake for about 8 minutes. Remove from oven and sprinkle with parmesan cheese. Place back in oven for an additional 8 minutes or until golden in color. Let cool completely. Keep croutons in airtight container until use.

# *Beef Stock*

*I often make my own stock for soups. It also freezes well for other uses like gravies or sauces. It takes a little effort to make but the difference in homemade and store bought is huge.*

**Makes about 1 quart**

2 llbs. Beef soup bones
2 lbs. combination beef and veal bones
¼ cup tomato paste
3 carrots cut into 2" pieces
3 celery stalks, cut into 2" pieces
2 medium onions, quartered
1 cup red wine
3 quarts water
Cheesecloth
4 parsley sprigs
2 thyme sprigs
2 cloves crushed garlic
3 bay leaves
10 whole black peppercorns

**Cook's Note**

To make a demiglace you will need to reduce the already reduced cooled stock. Let stock come to simmer and cook for another 2 hours or until it gets a little syrupy looking. When this cools it will look like a gelatin. Remove any fat which comes to the surface.

Preheat oven to 400 degrees. Place bones in single layer in a roasting pan. Brush with tomato paste. Roast for 45 minutes. Remove from oven and set bones aside. In the same roasting pan add carrots, celery and onions and reduce heat to 375. Put in oven for 35 minutes. Remove from oven and place roasting pan over 2 burners over medium heat. Stir vegetables scraping up bits from bottom of pan. Add wine to deglaze pan. Let wine reduce for about 3 minutes. In a large stock pot add bones, vegetables, and bits from pan. Add about 3 quarts cold water or enough to just cover bones. Make an herb sachet by placing parsley, thyme, garlic, bay leaves and peppercorns in a triple layer of cheesecloth. Gather edges up and tie with kitchen string, keeping one end of string longer. Place sachet in pot and tie the longer end to the pot handle. Simmer stock uncovered for 6 hours or up to 8 hours. Remove bones and strain liquid through colander into a large bowl. Strain again through a finer meshed strainer. Place bowl with stock into an ice bath to cool it down. As it cools the fat will rise to the surface and you can spoon it off or you can put the stock in the refrigerator overnight and spoon off the fat in the morning. You may freeze the stock by putting it in an ice cube tray. When frozen, wrap each cube separately. Use when needed.

#  Chicken Stock

*This is a basic chicken stock which can be frozen after it's cooked.*

**Makes about 3 quarts**

One 3-4 lb. chicken cut up
2 carrots, peeled, cut into ½" pieces
2 celery stalks, cut into ½" pieces
1 large onion, cut into ½" pieces
2 sprigs parsley
1 bay leaf
2 sprigs thyme
5-6 peppercorns
16 cups water

Place chicken and vegetables in a large stock pot. Add water. Bring to a boil. Put herbs in a double or triple layer of cheesecloth. Tie tightly with a string, keeping one end longer so you can hang it outside the stock pot. Place herbs in cheesecloth down into soup and tie the longer end to the handle. Reduce heat to a simmer and cook uncovered for 3 hours, skimming off the foam as it rises to the surface. Strain, discard chicken and vegetables and return the stock to the pot. Keep simmering until liquid is reduced by about half. Let cool and refrigerate until fat rises to surface and can be removed.

# *Slow Roasted Tomatoes*

*David, a good friend of mine, grows the most incredible vegetables. His tomatoes are award winning and thankfully he shares with friends. This is one of his recipes interpreted by me.*

**Makes 24**

12 medium ripe tomatoes, any variety
¾ cup **Tuscan Herb Extra Virgin Olive Oil**
1 Tbs. **Aged or Lavender Balsamic Vinegar**
3 cloves garlic, minced
1 tsp. dried thyme leaves
Kosher salt
Granulated sugar

Preheat oven to 250 degrees. Coat a 12 x 17 rimmed baking sheet with 2 Tbs. olive oil. Remove stems of tomatoes and cut in half horizontally. Place in a large bowl and add about ½ cup olive oil, balsamic, garlic and thyme. Mix gently. Place tomatoes cut side up on baking sheet. Sprinkle each half with a pinch of salt and a pinch of sugar. Pour remaining olive oil over and around tomatoes. Roast tomatoes for about 6 hours or until a dark reddish brown with brownish edges. Serve warm or room temperature.

**Cook's Note**
Don't throw out the tomato oil from the baking sheet. Save in a jar for vinaigrette or some other use. Tomatoes can be jarred or frozen for a longer freshness time. You can substitute 18 Year Aged Balsamic Vinegar for the Lavender Vinegar.

# Vinaigrettes

*Here are a few different vinaigrettes. The choice is endless. Use your own creativity to come up with some others. The directions are simple, add ingredients to a bowl and whisk.*

## Sesame Vinaigrette

1 Tbs. **Roasted Sesame Oil**
3 Tbs. rice wine vinegar
1 Tbs. soy sauce
3 Tbs. white sesame seeds, toasted
1 Tbs. **Honey Ginger Balsamic Vinegar**
1/3 cup water

## Lemon Tarragon Vinaigrette

3 Tbs. **Sicilian Lemon Balsamic Vinegar**
1 tsp. lemon zest, grated
1 Tbs. minced shallots
1 Tbs. minced tarragon
¼ cup **Tarragon Extra Virgin Olive Oil**
salt and pepper

## Chipotle Tangerine Vinaigrette

1/3 cup **Chipotle Extra Virgin Olive Oil**
2 tsp. grated orange zest
1 Tbsp. orange juice
½ tsp. dried oregano
½ cup **Tangerine Balsamic Vinegar**
1 tsp. ground cumin
Salt

## Strawberry Vinaigrette

2 Tbs. **Hojiblanca Extra Virgin Olive Oil**
1 Tbs. lemon juice
3 Tbs. **Strawberry Balsamic Vinegar**
1 tsp. Chopped fresh mint
Salt and pepper

## Lavender Vinaigrette

6 Tbs. **Arbosana Extra Virgin Olive Oil**
2 Tbs. **Lavender Balsamic Vinegar**
1 garlic clove minced
1 tsp. Dijon mustard

## Tuscan Herb Vinaigrette

4 Tbs. **Tuscan Herb Extra Virgin Olive Oil**
2 Tbs. **18 Year Aged Balsamic Vinegar**
2 Tbs. minced shallots
2 tsp. Dijon mustard
Salt and pepper

# *Balsamic Onion Marmalade*

*Use this on a sandwich, over grilled meats, roasted meats or on crostini's or cheese.*

**Makes 2 cups**

2 Tbs. **Herbs de Provence Extra Virgin Olive Oil**
1 Tbs. unsalted butter
2 red onions cut in half, sliced 1/8" thick
1 yellow onion cut in half, sliced 1/8" thick
½ cup dry red wine
¼ cup light brown sugar
½ teaspoon salt
¼ teaspoon ground pepper
1 ½ teaspoon minced fresh rosemary
1 ½ teaspoon chopped fresh thyme
¼ cup **18 Year Aged Balsamic Vinegar**

Melt butter and oil in a large saucepan over medium heat. Add onions and cook over medium heat for about 5 minutes, while stirring constantly. Add wine, brown sugar, salt and pepper, rosemary and thyme and bring to a boil, stirring constantly. Reduce heat to low and cover. Simmer about 40 minutes until onions are tender. Add vinegar and increase heat to medium high. Cook uncovered another 3-5 minutes, stirring occasionally until liquid is reduced to a thick glaze .Remove from heat and let cool. Place cooled marmalade in a covered bowl or jar. It can be stored in refrigerator up to one week. Bring to room temperature before serving.

#  *Balsamic Glaze*

*Any dark balsamic can be reduced to a syrupy glaze.  This can be used in many recipes and also to decorate plates when balsamic vinegar is in the recipe.*

**Makes ¼ cup**

1 cup flavored dark **Balsamic Vinegar**

Put vinegar in a small noncorrosive saucepan over medium heat.  Bring to a boil and immediately turn heat down.  Simmer uncovered until reduced by half.  This could take about 40 minutes.  Remove saucepan from heat and let sit until completely cooled.  Vinegar will thicken more as it cools.  Do not rush the process.  For a thicker glaze, continue reducing to ¼ cup.  Place in a lidded jar or plastic container.  No need to refrigerate.

**Cook's Note**
You can double the recipe.  The reducing time will be longer.  Always be careful not to have the heat too high, the vinegar will burn.  Keep in mind that the flavor of the balsamic is more concentrated and sweeter when you reduce it to a glaze.

**Footnote**
I like to keep the glaze in a plastic bottle with a capped thin tipped spout for easy pouring.

# *Lemon Herb Sauce*

*This is a very versatile sauce.  It is heated slightly and can be served, hot or at room temperature.  It will become one of your favorite sauces.*

**Makes 3/4 cup**

½ cup mild to medium **Extra Virgin Olive Oil** such as **Nocellara, Arbosana, Leccino**
¼ cup freshly squeezed lemon juice
1 clove garlic
1 Tbs. minced fresh parsley
½ tsp. salt, more if needed'
pepper

Peel garlic clove and crush with the side of the knife.  Add salt and make a paste.  Put olive oil in saucepan over medium, low heat.  Add lemon juice and mashed garlic and whisk.  Add parsley and continue whisking until heated through.  Serve sauce.

**Cook's Note**
Use this sauce on fish, chicken, vegetables or pasta.  Add 2 Tbs. of capers for a salty, sour taste.  You can use Eureka Lemon Extra Virgin Olive Oil in place of the olive oils suggested above.  Reduce the amount of lemon juice and test for taste.

# Candied Orange Peel

*The peels take about 2 days to dry. For a real treat dip dried peel in chocolate and lay on wax paper to dry.*

**Makes 2 cups**

2 large naval oranges, ¼ " off top and bottom
4 cups sugar
3 cups water

Cut orange peel into 4 vertical segments. Remove peels in one piece, scraping off as much pith, (the white part), as you can. Cut segments into ¼" wide strips. Boil water In a large saucepan and cook strips for about 15 minutes. Drain, and rinse strips. In another saucepan bring 3 cups sugar and 3 cups water to a boil, and stir to dissolve the sugar. Add the peels and return to boil. Immediately reduce heat and simmer until the peels are very soft, about 45 minutes. Drain. Toss peels with remaining one cup of sugar and lay strips on a baking sheet lined with foil. Let stand until coating on peels is dry, about 1 to 2 days. Wrap and freeze or store in an airtight jar until use.

Finished!

#  *Olive Oil and Balsamic Vinegar Pairings*

## Infused Olive Oils

## Balsamic Vinegars

Basil Organic Extra Virgin Olive Oil

Black Cherry, Blackberry Ginger, Fig, Peach, Cranberry Pear, Sicilian Lemon, Pomegranate, Strawberry

Blood Orange Extra Virgin Olive Oil

Blueberry, Cinnamon Pear, Dark Chocolate, Fig, Espresso, Pomegranate, Tangerine Sicilian Lemon, Cranberry Pear

Butter Extra Virgin Olive Oil

Cinnamon Pear, Blueberry, Maple, Pumpkin Spice, Coconut

Chipotle Extra Virgin Olive Oil

Dark Chocolate, Coconut, Peach, Espresso, Cranberry Pear, Jalapeno, Pineapple

Cilantro and Roasted Onion Extra Virgin Olive Oil

Lavender, Coconut, Oregano, Strawberry, Red Apple, Peach, Honey Ginger

Eureka Lemon Extra Virgin Olive Oil

Blackberry Ginger, Fig, Blueberry, Black Cherry, Raspberry, Strawberry,

Garlic Organic Extra Virgin Olive Oil

Black Cherry, Blackberry Ginger, Fig, Oregano, Peach, Apricot, Mango, Pineapple, Raspberry, Tangerine, Sicilian Lemon, Pomegranate, Red Apple, Jalapeno

Harissa Extra Virgin Olive Oil

Blackberry Ginger, Cinnamon Pear, Honey Ginger, Cranberry Pear, Tangerine, Raspberry Pineapple, Jalapeno

# Infused Olive Oils

Herbs de Provence Organic Extra Virgin Olive Oil

Milanese Gremolata Extra Virgin Olive Oil

Persian Lime Organic Extra Virgin Olive Oil

Porcini Extra Virgin Olive Oil

Tuscan Herb Organic Extra Virgin Olive Oil

Wild Mushroom and Sage Extra Virgin Olive Oil

All of the above Extra Virgin Olive Oils

# Balsamic Vinegars

Lavender, Blueberry, Cinnamon Pear, Sicilian Lemon, Raspberry, Strawberry, Blackberry Ginger, Fig, Grapefruit

Oregano, Sicilian Lemon, 18 Year Traditional, Grapefruit,

Black Cherry, Blackberry Ginger, Coconut, Dark Chocolate, Honey Ginger, Lavender, Raspberry, Mango, Apricot, Blueberry, Pomegranate, Strawberry, Cranberry Pear

Sicilian Lemon, Oregano, 18 Year Traditional

18 Year Traditional, Fig, Oregano, Peach, Raspberry, Tangerine, Espresso, Peach White Pomegranate, Sicilian Lemon

Black Cherry, Fig, Oregano, Sicilian Lemon, 18 Year Traditional

18 Year Traditional

**Footnote:** To make Vinaigrette: Use 1 part Balsamic Vinegar to 2-3 parts Extra Virgin Olive Oil
(For a sweeter, less calorie dressing, use 1 part oil to 2 parts vinegar)

To make a Marinade:  Use 1 part Balsamic Vinegar to 1 part Extra Virgin Olive Oil

# *Nut, Seed, and Other Oil Pairings*

## Oils

Roasted Almond Oil

French Walnut Oil

Roasted Sesame Oil

## Balsamic Vinegars

Raspberry, Cinnamon Pear, Cranberry Pear, Blueberry, Peach White, Strawberry, Dark Dark Chocolate, Espresso, Fig, Pomegranate

Cranberry Pear, Blackberry Ginger, Red Apple, Pumpkin Spice, Cinnamon Pear, Blueberry, Strawberry, Pomegranate

Coconut, Honey Ginger, Apricot, Tangerine, Sicilian Lemon

# Flavor Notes and Food Pairings for Extra Virgin Olive Oil

*There are many uses for extra virgin olive oil.  Below are a few different flavors and how to use them in your cooking*

## Delicate Extra Virgin Olive Oils

These have a mild, creamy, buttery taste with sweetness on the tongue:
**Arbequina, Nocellara Del Belice, Sweet Barnea and Hojiblanca**
Great for baking, broiled and grilled fish, steamed vegetables, mild cheeses, soups and mild sauces.

## Medium Bodied Extra Virgin Olive Oils

These have a fruity, olive taste described as grassy and flavors of apples or banana leaves:
**Arbosana, Manzanillo, Picual, and Favolosa**
Compliments grilled meats and vegetables, heavier sauces, pastas, bruschetta, and mild cheeses.

## Robust Extra Virgin Olive Oils

These have a spicy, fruity, peppery and pungent flavor:
**Picholine, Koroneiki, Cobrancosa and Coratina**
Compliments salads, sauces, risottos, grilled meats, bruschetta, pasta and rustic dishes.

# *Menu Planner*

The following menus are merely suggestions. My favorite part of cooking is preparing a coherent menu. Start with an appetizer, go into a light salad, pick your entrée and finish with a dessert. The rule of thumb is if you have a rich entrée' then keep your dessert light. If you have a lighter entrée you can have a heavier dessert. Keep the portions light so you are not too full for dessert.

**Elegant Dinner Party**
Caprese Salad
Filet Mignon with Black Cherry Cabernet
Mashed Potatoes with Truffle Oil
Beet, Orange and Walnut Salad
Crepes with Balsamic Berries

**Friday Night Dinner Party**
Radicchio and Red Cabbage Salad
Salmon with Orange Champagne Glaze
Garlic Roasted Potatoes
Spinach Soufflé
Tangy Cheesecake with Berry Coulis

**Light Dinner**
Shrimp Scampi Pasta
Almond Oil Lemon Cake

**Summer Dinner Party**
Fig Tapenade and Mascarpone Crostini
Bruschetta over Breaded Pork Cutlets
Salad with Vinaigrette
Peach Tart with Vanilla Ice Cream

**Italian Dinner**
Roasted Tomato, Pesto, Goat Cheese Torta
Caesar Salad
Broccoli Rabe and Sausage Pasta
Tiramisu

**Wine and Appetizer Party**
Marinated Olives
Melon and Proscuitto
Onion Balsamic Brie
Deviled Eggs with truffle Oil
Sausage and Leek Tart
Pumpkin Butter and Goat Cheese Crostini
Crab Cakes with Two Aioli's
Assorted Cheeses
Assorted Wines

**Taco Night**
Guacamole and Chips
Fish Tacos with Slaw and Curried Mayo
Tomato and Roasted Corn Salsa
Coconut Ambrosia

Just for fun I included this menu. I made an Italian dinner after I came back from Tuscany. I was so impressed by the food there. By the way, everything had olive oil on or in it! I did not have any of these dishes but have added my own version. I have tried to translate into Italian and hope I did so correctly.

# *Tuscan Menu*

## Passata di pomadoro su pane
*Tomato puree on Toasted bread*

## Tagliatelle alla norcina a funghi
*Sausage and mushroom pasta*

## Pollo Involtini
## con
## potate al forno
*Rolled chicken with roasted potatoes*

## Pan di spagna al limone
## con fruitti bosco
*Lemon sponge cake with berries*

## Espresso

# Safe Cooking Temperatures Chart

| Protein | Internal Temperature | |
|---|---|---|
| Beef | 145 degrees | Medium Rare |
| | 150 degrees | Medium |
| | 170 degrees | Well Done |
| Pork | 145 degrees | |
| Cooked Hams | 140 degrees | |
| Turkey, Chicken, Duck | | |
| Stuffed | 165 degrees | |
| Unstuffed | 180 degrees | |
| Fish (Fin Fish) | 145 degrees | |

# Conversion Chart

| Butter/Margarine | to | Olive Oil |
|---|---|---|
| 1 teaspoon | | ¾ teaspoon |
| 1 tablespoon | | 2 ¼ teaspoons |
| 2 tablespoons | | 1 ½ tablespoons |
| ¼ cup | | 3 tablespoons |
| 1/3 cup | | ¼ cup |
| ½ cup | | ¼ cup + 2 tblsp. |
| 2/3 cup | | ½ cup |
| ¾ cup | | ½ cup + 1 tblsp. |
| 1 cup | | ¾ cup |

Making Stuffed Cannelloni with Mama Mimmi in Tuscany

# *Index*

# Index (cont'd)

# Index (cont'd)

# Index (cont'd)

# Index (cont'd)

# Index *(cont'd)*

# Notes